# Lessons Learned On A
# *Broken Road*

Written by:
## MYA SPAULDING

*Lessons Learned On A Broken Road*

Copyright 2026 by Mya Spaulding

All rights reserved. This book or any portion thereof may not be reproduced or used in any manner whatsoever without the express written permission of the publisher except for the use of brief quotation in a book review.

Because of the dynamic nature of the Internet, any web addresses or links contained in this book may have changed since publication and may no longer be valid.

ISBN: 978-1-971439-01-3 (sc)

"Parents, your words to your children will echo through their minds for the rest of their lives."

    Author Spaulding presents an emotive memoir of her chaotic, dramatic life journey sustained by her spiritual outlook at every twist and turn. Born to a poor farm family and the middle child, she was adored, guided, and dominated by her outgoing, somewhat overbearing father but rejected by her lonely, withdrawn mother, who had not wanted a second child. As a result, the author soon learned to work and to obey, her youthful zest and intelligence noticeable in her quick grasp of farm chores, her love of animals, and her genuine interest in all things mechanical. Beset by measles and a dangerously high fever at age five, she developed a lifelong disorder that caused weight gain and hair loss, requiring her to wear a wig and suffer taunts from other children.

US Book Review by<br>Barbara Bamberger Scott

# DEDICATION

I dedicate this book to my Lord and Savior for His glory and honor. I could never earn or deserve the blessings He has given me. I thank my children - His greatest blessings to me other than salvation - for their love and patience over the years. You have walked through the fires with me and still love me. You have been my reason to keep getting up and trying again. You forgave me for my failures. I thank God for all of you daily. And, a special thank you to my son Joey for choosing the title of this book.

# GUARD RAILS

I remember standing on the transmission tunnel of Dad's 1952 Dodge pickup truck, so I could see out the window, and noticed the guard rails. I asked, "Daddy, what are they, and why are they there?"

Dad said, "They are guard rails and are put over rivers and steep slopes so people "don't go over a cliff or land in a river. We don't want people to get hurt or wreck their trucks. The smooth, level places don't need them because if someone did go off the road there, they may be shaken up, and the vehicle may have a few "dings and dents" but probably would be ok."

"Guard rails" in life help guide and protect all who travel life's roads. The problem is we children - are not taught what "Life's Guard Rails" are. We make mistakes that can't be reversed, and leave many mental, physical, and emotional scars that have lifelong hurts, regrets, and shame.

Lessons Learned on a Broken Road tells the real-life story of how one broken life was renewed, and I pray - shows how to avoid the "going over the cliff and wrecking the truck" situations. Even if you think that your life is a totally unfixable train wreck, it can be repaired and hearts can be healed. Your life can be renewed. Never give up. Never quit. The Light still shines at the end of the tunnel. There is always hope. You are loved, you are precious, your life can still be renewed.

# INTRODUCTION

As with most people, there have been many moments in my life when I wondered why God had even bothered to make me. I felt that I was a total and complete failure. "I can't do anything right", making the same mistakes over and over again. Then – my entire life changed, through His amazing mercy and grace. As I reached my sixtieth birthday, I began to wonder who God had intended me to be, and what His purpose and plans still hold.

Putting my life, as I have seen it, on paper may help sort this out. Beauty may be in the eye of the beholder, but reality is in the beholder's mind.

A few years ago, while conversing with friends, a unique perspective arose. One wondered if perhaps our life journey isn't as much about becoming "something", but perhaps about "unbecoming" the things that we were not intended to be… and letting go of unnecessary baggage. When I turned 60, I began to wonder who God had originally designed me to be, and what His purpose and plans still hold. Putting my life on paper, as I have seen it, may help sort things out. As I ponder the path my life has taken, I realize how much our childhood home environment influences and shapes us. For better or worse – I truly thank God for my family. Without them, I would not be the person I am today.

This book is first and foremost - dedicated to my Lord and Savior – for His glory and honor. I could never earn or deserve the blessings that He has given me. I want to thank all my children, His greatest blessings to me - other than salvation - for their love and patience over the years. You have walked through the fires with me and still love me. You have been my reason to keep getting up and trying again. You forgave me for my failures. I thank God for you daily.

I was born in late December 1954 to struggling parents who could barely afford to breathe. The effects of the depression were alive and well. The local bank had closed their doors, and the depositors lost everything. I heard, many times, my grandfather recall being part of the crowd gathered there, pounding on the doors, trying to get in. They could see the staff inside, motioning for the people to go away. Everything was gone. Not a penny was left. After many hours of anger, frustration, panic, tears, and fear, they turned away for a long, sad ride home.

This was something they never forgot. An indelible memory forever etched into the very core of their survival. Many families had lost their farms, but by the grace of God, our neighborhood survived. I remember the cooperation of the close-knit families. One owned a corn shredder and brought it to everyone who needed it. The men worked from one farm to the next until all the corn was harvested. When it was our turn, I spent the days carrying ice cold water in a bucket, straight from the well, to the hot, hardworking men while Mom and Grandma cooked a big noon meal.

Our beautiful farm had been purchased in the early 1900's by my grandmother with a small inheritance from her family. She and two sisters came from southern Minnesota and bought neighboring farms. They married, and with their husbands, bought additional land, which created a mostly Swedish heritage valley. Grampa was an excellent barn builder, so every farm had a sturdy, beautiful home for their cattle.

Several years later her brother bought a fourth farm on the same road. They struggled together to build barns, carve fields out of forests, and keep the wells flowing. Many hours of hard manual labor fueled by a great love of the land carried them through and gave them a focus. My father was born to them quite late in life. My Grandmother was nearly forty years old and had given up hope of having a child of her own. He was her gift from God, and she doted on him to the extent of re-cooking an entire meal if it wasn't what he wanted. If she had made a roast and he wanted chicken, Grandpa would go out and butcher a chicken. Chores would wait until their son was content. They didn't have much to give him materially, but their only child, born later in life 'ruled the roost'. To her, he was a gift from God, and she gave him everything she had to give.

We lived on my grandparent's farm in a house that Grandpa and Dad had built out of home cut lumber, with cousins and neighbors providing additional labor, supplies, and advice. We didn't have running water (unless running to the pump house with a bucket counts) and cooked on a wood stove with a warming closet and a reservoir. The house was heated with a pot-bellied stove in the living room. This became quite interesting when someone accidentally put a piece of maple wood in it. The top – complete with the full tea kettle – would blow off! It became a huge mess of hot water, smoke, ashes, and cinders!!!

The upstairs was so cold on frigid winter nights that my older sister and I would put our clothes in the bed between us, so they wouldn't be freezing cold in the morning. The frost on the inside of the windows could be half an inch thick.

Praise God - we had electricity!!! Ours was one of the last homes in the neighborhood to get 'modern plumbing' and a telephone. But - it was our home, and I loved it. When I was nine, Dad built an addition onto the house, and we eventually became blessed with an electric stove, a kitchen sink, and a real bathroom!! No one missed that outhouse at all! I still thank God for making people smart enough to make water heaters and showers!

Money was hard to come by, and saving it was harder. We learned very early to be frugal and to 'make do' with what we had. Dad said, "Necessity is the mother of invention". We became very creative with what we had. "Waste not... Want Not..." When my parents were married, milk was selling for $4.50/hwt. Dad had calculated how to provide for a wife and child on that income level. He hadn't counted on a second child or a drastic decrease in their income. By the time I was born, it had gone down to $3.00/hwt. At this writing, it is approximately $16/hwt. Dwight Eisenhower was president and, as today, inflation was a problem. And there was no public assistance. Dad felt that he had to "run a tight ship" to provide for our family.

A low income, balancing a new marriage, scraping together enough resources to build a house, in-law issues and an unwanted pregnancy – me – created unending sources for dissention. I thank God that abortion wasn't available then, because I know that I would have been murdered. I would never have known how wonderful life can be. My children, grandchildren – and a beautiful great granddaughter - wouldn't exist. A horrifying thought… (As I look back at God creating me and keeping me alive, having heard my parents talking about it, I ponder the phrase, "my body… my choice…," I have always wondered, "If it was MY body, wouldn't it be called "suicide"???) Thank You Lord for holding me tight in the palm of Your hand!

My older sister managed to escape a great deal of uncomfortable situations because Grandpa and Grandma loved her dearly and kept her most of the time. If Dad or Mom wanted her home, they sent me to get her. This was never news well received. I had to knock before entering, state my business and leave. They referred to me as "Slop Mya", a rather uncomplimentary term. (In the days of no running water, there was always a 'slop' bucket in the kitchen…)

I was not welcomed in their home. They had one child. They had one grandchild. That was all they wanted. There was no need or desire for a second one. I knew that and accepted it. There were no other options. It was ok. I think that I was born knowing 'It is what it is. I can't fix it or change it'. Do the best you can with what you have and keep walking. I was born knowing that if someone didn't want you, or love you, standing on your hands and walking backwards was never going to change anything. I learned from a very early age to be quiet, obedient, and do not, under any circumstances, make waves. The term 'compliant' was a description of ideal behavior to keep my home as peaceful as possible. "Adapt, overcome, keep walking."

My place of peace was the "forty"- the forty-acre parcel of land that my Grandfather purchased after he and Gramma were married in 1910. It was on the south side of the dirt road. This was the "day pasture" for the milk cows. There was a "dry run" which ran hard in the spring with the snow melting, and sometimes in the summer, slowed down to a trickle depending on the amount of rainfall. There was wildlife and birds of many different kinds, clusters of beautiful butterflies, swarms of bumblebees and honeybees, meandering cow paths through big, beautiful trees, and peaceful rolling hills covered with wildflowers and thick green grass. And three ponds with the cutest toads and frogs! It was fascinating to watch tadpoles hatch and develop into frogs that could sing all night. How amazing is God's glorious creation! The closest place to "Heaven on earth" that I have ever seen.

On the summer days when Dad had to go somewhere and I couldn't go with him, Mom would shut me out of the house. She would tell me to go outside and play. When I became strong enough to toddle that distance, I would head up the hill to "the forty". There were my cows, and God's peace. They would hear me coming and come to meet me. I would spend the day there with them. I was safe, loved, and protected. And in total complete peace. Sometimes, I would fall asleep with a cow laying beside me. On my way up there, I would try to sneak some corn from the corncrib into my pocket so I could feed a couple of chipmunks out of my hand. They are soooo cute.

When Dad would come home, I could hear him yell, "Where in the world is MYA???" Voices tended to echo through the whole valley! Mom would say that she didn't know, because she honestly had no idea. Soon, I'd hear Dad running up to the gate calling my name. I would try to toddle to meet him, and he would pick me up, make sure that I was ok, put me on the back of a cow, and we'd all go home. The "forty" was the rock of my entire first twenty years, and my mental haven of peace after life took me from it. There was never a more beautiful, peaceful place on this earth that I have ever seen. This was my heart's earthly home.

I believe that my mother may have loved her first-born child. But, since she was rather young, my paternal grandparents felt that Mother was incapable of caring for a baby. They didn't consider the fact that Mom had younger sisters whom she helped care for, besides neighbors and cousins that she had babysat and cared for since their births. Mother wanted her baby and so did Grandma. If Mom couldn't have her first child, she wanted nothing to do with a second one. Or perhaps so drug down and depressed by her life situation that she was emotionally spent with nothing left to give.

Years later, after my son was born, she told me "I had held out hope that you would have been a boy. When the doctor said that you were a girl, I wanted to cry. Then…. Your Dad walked over to the bassinet, put his hand down to you and you reached up and curled your little hand around his finger, and 'gurgled and cooed'. He smiled, and loved you, and I hated you." I said, "Mom, it's ok. I understand. I love you and I am so thankful for you." One time, years later when I told her I loved her, she said, "You can't love me." I smiled at her and said, "Yes I can, and you can't stop me…" She just turned away.

I recently learned that the neighboring ladies had an informal rotating schedule of 'visiting' for the purpose of checking on me to "make sure that you were still alive". To this day, I thank God for their love and concern. I can fully understand how sad, lost, and hurt Mother would have been. Dad wasn't all that interested in a crying baby and sleepless nights, plus, he wanted his parents to be content, so he wouldn't have to move. He didn't want to leave the home farm where he was born and raised. So……. Grandma won. Hands down. This was not a peaceful marital decision by any means.

Friction creates heat, and eventually, builds up into hurtful words that can't be erased. Apologies may be offered, but scars remain forever…. We had an old round oak dining room table. I remember sitting under it singing old hymns to myself to drown out the loud voice of my Dad, with Mom tearfully trying to defend herself from accusations and criticisms. The old ringer washer sat in the kitchen. The smells of Fels-Naptha soap, the squeaking of the ringer, and the sadness of my mother cannot be forgotten. She had no desire to be a wife or a mother.

The summer after I turned three, I had figured out how to do the dishes. Mom was not fond of doing them, so I relieved her of it as often as I could. After meals, I would drag a dining room chair to the wood cookstove and dip out the warm water from the reservoir for rinsing, fill one dishpan, then go back, lift the tea kettle full of hot water down on to the chair, slide it carefully to the counter where the dish pans sat and fill the other pan. Dad would say, "Good grief Mya! Be careful…", and I was.

Mom said, "You learned to walk and talk early, and you haven't sat down or shut up since. Your first word was 'Dada', the next thing was, 'Me do it'." Some things never change… In my preschool years, it seemed that most of the food we ate was flavored with the salt of her tears as she cried and stirred pots and pans on the old wood stove. I always tried to lighten her load.

I discovered early at about three years old, how to open the door to sweet peace. In this amazing place were approximately 27 big, soft, sweet, gentle momma cows and their calves of various ages. They didn't yell. They didn't argue. They loved unconditionally, like great big puppies. I knew I was loved and safe. I could snuggle up next to one and she would turn her head and hold me. This was my haven of peace, and they were my reason to live. I remember lying on the feed sacks in front of the manger, crying because I knew that if I were to die, no one would ever miss me or care. Then, a sweet soft nose reached out to nuzzle me, and pulled gently on my coat until I was next to her. She held me tight to her with her neck until I quit crying and slept.

Lord, I still thank You to this day for that cow. I remember standing looking at a cow's face, (her head was nearly as long as I was tall!!!) in total awe and wonder that God could make this amazing creature. All loving and giving - full of innocent trust. Huge soft eyes with long curly eyelashes blinking slowly. And – very few things are sweeter than a newborn baby calf! And their breath smells so sweet! These great big puppies even love to play with a big ball! (Pastor Kenny – you were so very wrong. When you described a stable as a dirty, stinky, unsuitable place for a baby, I couldn't disagree more. I could never imagine a better place for the Son of God to be born. When someone would ask me if I was born in the barn, I remember thinking "I could only wish…") Man has committed sins and transgressed all God's laws. Animals haven't sinned or transgressed a single one.

My precious cows were my whole world as a child. My sister was frequently with our grandparents during chores, so Dad always took me with him to the barn. When I was still a baby, he would put a small blanket on Teeny's back. Cradled by her hip bones, I laid there and slept during milking. Once I became a toddler, I couldn't be corralled. I was all over the barn. Once, Dad said that when I was trying to cross a gutter, I slipped and fell under a cow. She moved her foot, felt me, and held her foot up, and mooed loudly until Dad ran to pick me up! And away I went! I would do anything to help Dad take care of them.

I carried my own little shovel, full of feed, to them as soon as I could walk. I followed Dad everywhere and learned everything I could about the farm, from the birthing of calves to feed rations, building maintenance, machinery operation, crop production, and fencing. I would carry the staple can for him and drop it at nearly every post. He would wait patiently for me to pick them up and help if I was too slow! If only I had a nickel for every time he had said, "Good grief Mya …"

(He also hid my little pink baby mice from Mom so she couldn't feed them to the cat.)

I never realized until a few years ago that with my sister at Grandpa's and me with Dad, Mom was alone... She had no one. She had very little contact with her side of the family since they had moved to another state. She had grown up with a totally different lifestyle, values, familial background, financial status, and ways of handling situations. She liked "to go places and do things", but when the cows must be milked morning and night, and watched over like children, there wasn't much spare time to do that sort of thing. And, at that point in their marriage, he simply couldn't afford it.

The environment that we grow up in, is what we base our definition of "normal" on. All our basic values, and life expectations are deeply rooted. It is also a template for interactions with others, how we see ourselves, and acceptable lifestyles. For example, if you grew up in a high-rise apartment in New York City, you would have a very different way of thinking, processing daily needs, life expectations, methods of acquiring essentials, and handling situations than I do. The first few years of our life become a screen for sifting right from wrong, and building a lifelong foundational value system, in addition to meeting daily basic survival needs.

When I was in seventh grade, Dad was able to start taking Mom to "big city entertainments" where she could dress up and not look like a farmer's wife. I was old enough to take care of things overnight, and watch my little sister. I'd pick her up and put her and some toys in an empty calf pen where she'd play with the kittens while I milked the cows and did the rest of the chores. So, for a few days, Mom would be happy....

When we were home, I would try to make Dad laugh and distract him to ease her pressure. She told me years later that she didn't understand what I was trying to do for her from age three and on. She asked me, "Why didn't you tell me?" I said that I thought she knew. She had no bond with me and thought that I was trying to take Dad's attention away from her. That was my first realization that to her, any attention from him was better than no attention at all. I was thinking - *Peace at any price.*

There was a lot of work to be done, and by the time we were five years old, we needed to be able to milk 3 cows by hand. Our first cow was Little Holstein. Being patient and very gentle, she was a great place to start. We had one milking machine and Dad ran that. My mother, my sister, and I milked the rest by hand. My beautiful, amazing, tiny, little grandmother could milk more cows than all of us. This was the woman who broke all the horses in the area, especially the "wild" ones that none of the men could handle! They would bring them to her! Her own saddle horse would bow down on his knees, so Gramma could get on her side-saddle without messing up the long skirts that she always wore. She cried when the last horse passed, and the farms transitioned to cars, trucks, and tractors.

The love for, and wellbeing of the land and cattle was demonstrated and ingrained in us from the time we were born. Both grandparents were still coming out to help with barn chores when they were in their late 70's. Mom, my sister and I, and Grandma all rotated barn duties, depending on what else needed to be done. When I was older – fourth or fifth grade, Dad bought a second milker. By then, I was strong enough to lift the full ones and empty them safely.

My sister was never fond of the cattle, the smells, and the physical labor that was involved in farming and Grandma tried to shield her from as much as possible. I did learn an unforgettable lesson from her. One day she had to milk a cow she detested more than the others. I heard her talking in a soft, soothing tone to this poor scared creature. She was petting her gently to keep the cow calm and from kicking. I was quite impressed! But when I came close enough to hear the words she was saying I was stunned! In a very sweet, consoling tone of voice she was saying, "You are a rotten, worthless piece of garbage… If only I could grind you up into hamburger…." I guess that was the first time I realized how important tone of voice is. But it made me sad for poor little Rosebud!

I got an interview many years later because my supervisor had to know what kind of person would put 'can milk a cow' in the 'other skills and abilities' list…. I got the job!!

Back in the mid 50's to early 60's there were measles of every kind, chicken pox and mumps were very common. Not pleasant…. but common. And I think we had every kind of measles at least twice – or so it seemed. In June of 1960, a life changing event occurred. I came down with the German measles. At five and a half years old, my temperature was over 105 degrees, and stayed there for five or six days. Dad had called the local doctor, and he said to "let it run its course." I went in and out of consciousness – mostly out. At one point, I remember Dad telling Mom "I think that Mya is going to die." Before I passed out again, I heard Mom say, "I couldn't care less.", as she left and slammed the door behind her on her way out. She really didn't care. I don't recall anything for days after that. Mom wasn't feeling well either, and the barn chores still had to be done. That left her and Grampa to do it. Dad was afraid to leave me for very long for fear that I would die. At the same time, a new silo was being built. The crew of young men were very thoughtful and concerned about me. They would take turns coming in to check on me when Dad had to go outside to help or make decisions. When the silo was completed, one of the crew put his sunglasses on me and carried me outside to see their masterpiece. It was a wonderful and needed addition to our farm.

Our local doctor didn't seem to think it was a problem at all, but it left me permanently, physically changed. I lived by the grace of God, and life went on.

School was a place where I went, sometimes enjoyed or mostly endured while I was there, and grateful to come home from. I remember running straight from the kindergarten bus to Dad on a tractor and driving it for him, so he could load the hay bales onto the wagon. And getting off the bus to bring the cows home from "the forty", picking wildflowers for Mom on the way whenever I could find them. Even dandelions were welcomed but she loved buttercups. They were very difficult to reach since they only grew in the swamps. I remember always helping Dad plant the corn and oats. I either rode on the tractor with him or sat on the planter. We still used the old horse drawn planter that had been converted to fit on the hydraulic arms of our smallest narrow front-end tractor. I loved watching how the seeds came out so orderly, spaced perfectly, and knew that they would grow and become a beautiful field of feed for our cattle.

I had been given a baby kitten from a wonderful uncle when I was four. Every day when I got off the bus, she would come to meet me, and I would pick her up and she would ride on my shoulder back to the house. On the rare nights that I did not ride the bus home, Mom or Dad would have to lock Poppers in the barn, so she didn't freeze solid waiting for me. One cold winter night they forgot, and her ears were frozen off. She spent the rest of her precious life with little, short, rounded off ears.

This same uncle who lived across the road from us, had a brilliant black Lab, named… "Blacky". Blacky loved to play with my sister and me. If we were outside in the winter, and he could come over, he'd come running! When there was enough hard packed snow to go sliding, Blacky would wait until we were both seated safely, and checked to see that we had the rope in our hands. Then, he would run back behind us about 12 feet, and come flying towards us, jump on the sled and the inertia of his jump would send us all flying down the hill! Then, he would pull the sled back up the hill! He would happily play with us for hours. One time Dad was being mischievous and sat down on the sled behind me. Blacky stared at him, tipping his head from side to side, trying to figure out this strange situation. Then he sat down and barked at Dad until he got off, and we were all laughing so hard, that we fell off the sled halfway down the hill! When we were a little older, we learned to ski behind the tractor. Dad would run our WD45 down the country road where there was very little traffic, and, boy, did that thing fly! This was my older sister's most enjoyable winter fun! I much preferred Blacky's company and the sled.

We started first grade in a small, two room country school, where we went until I began fifth grade. My older sister and I were blessed with that school. There were three students in each grade, except hers. There were five of them. (She had the big class, in the big room…) We were blessed with excellent teachers and a lot of personal attention. All the students were "country kids", most were farming, and we all had similar lives – more or less. There was a peaceful commonality there. We took pride in how hard we could work, seeing the fruits of our labors in the growing crops, strong healthy baby calves, and selling the milk from healthy, pasture fed, contented cows. We enjoyed big swings, merry-go-rounds, slides, trampolines, and trees to climb. And, seeing how high we could swing, how fast we could spin, how high we could bounce, how fast we could run, and how high we could climb! Good times, great exercise, and a whole lot of fun!

There was a huge love of God and country. It was a clean, pure, American way of life. We knew that our families, a generation or more back, had immigrated to America to build a new life in freedom with opportunities. We were "American". And, "American" ends with "I CAN", not "I can't". We all knew it and valued it. I wouldn't change how I grew up even if I could. It gave us strength, taught us to evaluate a situation and handle it. Dad called it "self- starter" skills. See what needs to be done - and know how to do it. We learned how to figure things out for ourselves.

I do remember one time when Dad wasn't so happy with my curiosity about how things worked, and my knowledge of tools. He had gone to a farm supply store about 40 miles away and bought a very expensive new electric fencer because our old one had quit. I was about 6 years old, and watched him plug it in. All the lights lit up and flashed, reminding me of Christmas tree lights. He unplugged it and went into the house…

Well…. it was beautiful and I was fascinated. Sooo…. I climbed up on a block of wood, got a flathead and a Phillips screwdriver, and a couple of small wrenches, and began to try to find out what "made that thing tick…" And, to my horrified surprise, he came back out and seen his new expensive essential piece of equipment in pieces all over the floor. The look on his face was not good. He was speechless for a minute while trying to digest the situation. Then, he looked at me and said, "You put that thing back together RIGHT NOW. And it had better work when you're done!!!"

I didn't know how to pray, but God's hand must have been on me because, even though I had one tiny screw left over GLORY TO GOD, the fencer worked perfectly! And it continued to work beautifully for many, many years! And every time I'd go into the shed to turn it on, I'd start to laugh! I never told him about the leftover screw for many years! Then, we both laughed.

We had beautiful Christmas programs at our school, and Easter celebrations, and were blessed with all the parents' involvement. Mom had planted beautiful Dahlias, Gladiolas, Irises, and additional annual flowers around the school building, and the landscape was beautiful, and Dad provided hay wagons for hayrides, and parade events. I remember running in from the barn, washing up quickly, sliding into my other pair of pants, jumping in the truck, running down the stairs into the school basement just in time to climb up the ladder so my head would appear over the top of the huge Christmas tree and sing "Silent Night". It went well, and I didn't fall off the 10' ladder! Thank You Lord!!!!

I only had two pairs of pants, "wash" and "wear". I had to wash one pair in an old tub, and hang it over a chair back by the stove and pray that they'd be dry when I needed them in the morning. Thankfully, Grampa and Gramma provided my older sister with beautiful clothes and shoes, whenever she wanted them. I was always happy for her. This issue was far more important to her than me. What is in our heart is important, not the clothes we wear…. Like my Granddaughter would say, "Just keep that mess covered up…."

This is the place where I first heard the word "race" that didn't involve speed or an election. I didn't understand it then and I don't understand it now. God made flowers in all colors, shapes, and sizes. Put together, they make a gorgeous, fragrant bouquet! Much better together than alone! We had farm cats of all different colors, sizes, patterns, etc. All beautiful and loved for who they were. We had Holstein cows, Brown Swiss cows, Guernsey cows, Jerseys, and Milking Shorthorns. All different colors and personalities, some with spots and stripes. They all got along well, and functioned together as a herd protecting each other, and me. All equally amazing, and treasured. All birds are not the same size, shape, and color. Nothing is. God made a beautiful world out of individuals, with different gifts, who working together, can make a beautiful life with, and for each other. What color is your heart? White with fear, black with bitterness, red with anger, green with envy…… Heart color is far more important than skin color.

Then the teacher said that America is a "melting pot". I had watched enough welding to know what extreme heat does to metals. I questioned that because "if you take gold, silver and copper – which are all beautiful and valuable by themselves, and melt them down and stir, wouldn't it just become an unrecognizable mess?" But – when you make a stew, for example, every ingredient is very recognizable in the end product. Every ingredient compliments and brings out the best flavors and textures of the others. The end results of everyone working together are far better than one standing alone.

I grew up with no television in our house. And I was very thankful for that! There was no time to waste watching it and - I couldn't figure out if we were breathing people in or not. One night, when I was about four, we were at our neighbor's home, and they were watching a "western" movie. I asked my Godfather, "Who is that man?" He said, "John Wayne." Then I asked, "How did John Wayne get into that box?" He said that they were on waves in the air. I sure didn't want one of those things in our house.... And I really didn't want to inhale John Wayne....

Dad always said, "Life is not a spectator sport. It is a participation event. If you like baseball (as an example) – go play it! You are cheering for people you don't even know, that probably aren't even from the city, state, or college state that they play for. Everyone is making millions and you are just sitting there paying for it with your hard-earned money and your health. Get up and go do it yourself!!" And – we did! All the neighborhood kids, some parents, – and Mom and Dad! Badminton, volleyball, and Cow pie baseball! (Definitely not for the faint of heart!) "That one is first, that one is second ...there's third... and "Slide into home base at your own risk!!!!!" A great time was had by all!

By the time I was in second grade, my hair had started to thin and fall out. Dad took me to the local doctor. He attributed the problem to my fever having been way too high for way too long, but he had no idea what to do. I was sent to a much larger hospital, where they agreed about the cause, but again, no solution for the problem was found. My weight slowly began to rise. I was told that my thyroid gland had also been seriously affected – "burned out". I felt okay, but knew I wasn't like everyone else anymore. Every couple of weeks, Dad had to drive past our school to go into town to get our cattle feed ground, and get groceries and supplies, so if Mom wasn't with him, he would always stop and pick me up to ease my situation and keep me off the bus. At that time, he had a 1952 Dodge pickup. That truck was tough! It could go through thick heavy clay-based mud so deep that it was over the running boards. The previous owner had installed a delightful hood ornament. It was a small bull's head, and if the headlights were on, the eyes lit up bright red! So, I'd stand on the "transmission tunnel" by the floor mounted manual shift handle. Then I could see better out the windows. I was probably in second grade when Dad would push the clutch in and let me shift it for him! And not grind the gears, smoothly, and gently….

I loved going with Dad to the feed mill and watching the process. When I was little, we had to shovel all our corn and oats out of the pickup box into a big grinder and then supplemental vitamins and minerals were added, mixed well, and came down a pipe into gunny sacks, quickly tied with twine, tossed onto a conveyor belt and sent out to the farmer to load up and take home. The kind gentleman who operated the grinder loved my fascination for this process. One time when I was around three years old, he looked at me and said, "Come here!" Since I knew him well, I quickly ran to him. He tossed a sack of feed on the belt and put me on too! He stuck his head out and yelled to Dad, "Be careful with the next one!!!" Dad looked back, seen me and started to laugh so hard that he could hardly get me off the belt!!! He set me down on the floor, and I ran back in, and was placed back on the belt until Dad was fully loaded. This continued until I was too big to ride. This was the same sweet man who several years later protected me when I was in eighth grade. Mom was sick and required surgery. She had a hard time, and a long recovery. She was unable to do much of anything, so I had to fill her shoes. I had to do what I usually did plus what she did. Plus "the baby" was getting bigger and needed more attention. I had to do chores before I could go to school. And all the housework. Laundry, cooking, cleaning, etc. So. The only way I could get to school on time was to drive the truck into town and leave it at the feed mill. And make a hasty shortcut through a hilly wooded area. He knew the entire situation, as did the town police officer, and they covered me. They all knew the necessity and the situation.

One day when I was in town with Dad, I seen a man who looked like he was staggering and having trouble walking. I said, "Daddy! We need to stop and help him! He's going to fall down!" Dad sadly said, "Mya, there's nothing we can do. He's drunk." I asked, "What's that?" So, he explained to me what alcohol is, and what it does to a mind and body. This was so hard to see. A precious life so hurting and broken. An image burned in my heart and mind forever. Many years later in college, we learned that there is a "low threshold gene" for addictions, drugs, alcohol, etc. and, we never know if we have it until we take the first drink. Or the first drug. Or watch the first "temptation in the wrong direction". Don't open a door that can't be closed. It will only leave you with a life of shame and regrets. Life is too short, and too amazing to ruin the rest of your life for something that is destructive to your mind, body, and soul. God has much better planned for each of His children.

The condition worsened until the beginning of fourth grade when I had to start wearing a wig. Oh… Dear Lord, help me… No one had ever seen one… I stuck out like a skunk in church. Was treated like one also. Lord, please forgive them- they didn't know what they were doing. Why are people mean when it is so much easier to be nice? But, at the end of the day, I got to go home – and all was well.

No matter what happened off the farm, at home, I was still me. The cows still loved and needed me, and they couldn't have cared less what I looked like. There was more work than ever that needed to be done. Early in the spring, Dad decided to build an addition onto the house. Carpentry was something I had never been involved with, so this was a whole new experience. I watched the basement space being dug out, and the dirt piled. It would be hauled away as time allowed. The forms were built, carefully laid, and firmly fastened together. Then a seemingly unending amount of cement mixed, poured, leveled, and carefully smoothed with trowels. Then came the laying of the cement blocks. Grampa had been running the cement mixer, which was powered by a belt on the tractor's flywheel. One day, he had to step away from his position, and knowing that the operation had to keep flowing smoothly or it wouldn't get done, I stepped up to the plate. After I had dumped the first mixer load down to Dad, I started to modify Grampa's recipe. I had carefully watched Grampa as he added one shovel full of this, another of that, and two shovels of the next, and water to achieve the correct consistency.

After Dad got my second modified batch, his head appeared and he said, "Where in the world is Pa???" I said, "He had to leave a while ago. What's wrong???", thinking I was going to be in trouble…. He said, "Absolutely nothing!!! What have you been doing to the cement??? It's smoother, it holds better, overall, better consistency and stronger." I told him what I did, and he said, "Keep it up." And that when Grampa came back, he could do something else because Dad much prefered my work.

The house progressed rapidly, working on it between barn chores and the essential field work. It was exciting, and I was learning a lot. Later in life, I learned that knowledge of how to do things are called "transferable skills", and we all need them badly. We never know from day to day what is going to pop up in "life happens" moments, that will have to be dealt with swiftly. What we know is valuable, and sometimes lifesaving. If we can do something ourselves, we don't have to pay someone else to do it and will know that it was done right the first time.

Late, one afternoon, Dad looked at me and said, "Well, Mya…. Do you want to do chores and milk the cows, or shingle the roof?" I thought about it for half a minute, and said, "Well Daddy, I already know how to do that, but I've never shingled a roof. So, I want to try it. But… You know that I'm afraid of heights, so I'm only going to go 2 feet from the edges. If I look over, I'll fall over. So, the ends are your department." He laughed and said, "That works". He showed me how the roofing tar worked, where the shingle nails went, and headed to the barn, and I climbed up the ladder. And by the grace of God, I didn't fall off, and had the south side done when they were finished with the chores! I did the north side the next day while Dad finished my "too close to the edge" shingles.

Later, that summer between third and fourth grade, Dad had hired an older man to do the plumbing and electrical work on the new addition. This man happened to be in the milkhouse when I had to go in there also. Having been taught to always be obedient and compliant, he robbed me of my innocence. He told me that I could tell no one. Ever. From then on, I was not the same. I seen myself as used, dirty, guilty, and ashamed. Add this to the feeling of already feeling substandard, rejected by the world, and lost, I accepted that I was of no value to anyone except my little sister, my Dad, and my cows. And God. But I didn't know that God would lead me and guide me if I asked. No one ever told me that, or how to reach Him, and I didn't know how to ask. Many winter nights after the milking was done, I'd bring in the sawdust from a shed behind the barn to bed the cows. I would stand, looking up at the sky, until I was getting close to frozen, watching the beautiful northern lights. Absolutely gorgeous! In total awe and wonder of the incredible magnificence, pondering the brilliance of God. I knew He was up there somewhere watching everything. I could feel His presence.

How did He ever think of all these things, and everything came together so perfectly! All these thousands of years later, brilliant, highly educated people are still trying to figure out what He did, how He did it, and what they can do with it. We call them "scientists" …. I remember hearing a "joke" many years ago. It went like this… God was being confronted by the devil. He said that he too could make a man. Just like the Bible says God did. God said to go ahead and try it. So, the devil reached down and picked up a handful of dirt. God said, "NOPE. Make your own dirt." Game over.

The Northern Lights always bring back memories of Christmas on the farm. The tree was lit, and gifts were opened on Christmas Eve because we were "up north". We were told that Santa started unloading the gifts on his way south because it was easier on the reindeer, lightening their load earlier.... Then he could fill the stockings with the things he picked up in the south on his way back to the North Pole. And... funny little deal... there were always oranges, grapefruit, peaches, and pears in the stockings.... Hmmmm....

BUT... before we could go to the house, our sweet cows who supported us with giving their milk were gifted with an extra scoop of grain, extra bedding, and all were curried, and petted with love and appreciation. Without the cows, we wouldn't be farmers.

Turning off the barn lights, walking out the door into the beautiful winter wonderland, seeing the beautiful bright stars in the sky, trying to see if I could see the star that led the Wise Men to baby Jesus, and hearing the crunch of frozen snow in the absolute silence of the night will never be forgotten.

Then Dad and I would join Mom, Grampa, Gramma, my sister, and my Godparents in the house to eat supper and open gifts. I usually got one toy – and new socks and maybe a pair of shoes. I was always so happy and thankful. The amount of the gifts or their cost didn't matter, it was the thought that someone cared enough to think of me that mattered. Grampa usually took my older sister and I somewhere to go shopping so we were able to give in return. The only thing about Christmas Eve that was not enjoyable at all, was that Mom always had to make oyster stew for supper. It was her family's tradition.... Gross. Beyond. Belief. My older sister – to this day, calls it "Goober Soup". Hate to admit it, but I definitely agree.... So, let's move on to New Year's Day dinner... Grampa, being Swedish, had to make lutefisk and lefse - his family's tradition. Consumption of that was way beyond my stomach's ability. Plus, it had to get past my nose....

In August, before fourth grade started, God gave me an amazing gift! A beautiful baby sister! The littlest, prettiest, most precious thing

I had ever seen! And again, Mom didn't want the second one – she sure didn't want to deal with a third one. After listening to the brand-new baby crying alone for a couple of nights, I quietly went downstairs, picked her up, fed her, changed her, and tucked her into bed with me. She slept there peacefully with me until I moved out of the house. I know this isn't recommended, but God worked it out for good for us. At nine and a half, my mother hen instincts were already full blown. I would get off the bus, run to the house, heat a bottle, feed, bathe, and change the baby. All before I went out to help with the barn chores. If I recall correctly, her formula was a recipe consisting of fresh milk, clear Karo syrup, a pinch of baking soda and a little water to dilute it.

Back then, the bottles were made of glass – no plastic. It only took one time to learn that I couldn't take a bottle out of the refrigerator and stick it in the hot tea kettle on the wood stove to warm. There was a loud cracking noise… the bottle shattered, and the precious hot water was ruined. Dad said a few loud words about me and my ignorance. I never did that again!!! And ladies – there were no such things as disposable diapers back then. Cloth diapers, pins, and plastic pants that leaked, more or less, depending on the importance of the occasion. The more important the occasion, the greater the odds of a leak in the middle of it! I dreaded weddings and funerals…. Oh, the joys… Clean out as much as you could, rinse in cold water carried in from the well house, scrub, soak in bleach, and rewash. Most were washed by hand. It was not practical to heat gallons of water to start the ringer washer. In the summer, they were hung on the clothesline, but in the winter, the clothesline went back across the living room. The children were potty trained much earlier for very good reasons. Might I mention – no disposable baby wipes either…

I recall one beautiful Sunday morning before church, I had dressed her so perfectly and sat her down on the lawn with her little white dress flounced out all around and the prettiest little white lace ruffied plastic pants. So, I just had to take her picture with Dad's old 'box' camera. Then, I picked her up to get into the car and realized that she had been sitting on a spot of chicken doo-doo……. So, back into the house – rewash – change- and out the door to church. And we weren't late, by the grace of God!!!

My earliest memories of church were rather unpleasant. My sister and I went with our grandparents into town to a denominational church that was mostly comprised of non-farmers. That was the first time I felt looked down upon. It was well made known that we were not 'city' kids. We were a lower social class. We dressed differently. They said that we "smelled" different. They avoided us like the plague. We weren't good enough. I asked them "What do you do all day?" They looked at each other, and said, "Nothing. Watch TV I guess." Well… you have my deepest sympathy. I wouldn't have traded my life for their emptiness at all. They never experienced the shock and fear of being chased by an older sister with a creepy horrid snake, only to be able to retaliate by holding a sweet fuzzy bumblebee in your hand and making her run screaming to Gramma's! So much for "tough"!!! Some friends from high school visited a while ago and brought it up and we all laughed hard for a long time!

The Sunday school was a torment due to the teasing about my hair, our clothes, our cows, and farming. Church was worse. It was 'ritual' not 'relationship' based. ("Let's turn to page 574 and read a prayer." Really??? And if you wanted to talk to your dad, you'd have someone write a letter, so you could read it to him??? Why don't you just talk straight to him???) And- we always sat behind an older, affluent couple who took great pride in their position in the church and community. One of the manifestations of this pride was that the wife always wore a dead animal wrapped around her neck, as a status symbol. No matter the season - this dead, big buggy eyed, pitiful critter always stared at me through the whole service. One of those, that even if I moved, it looked like the big buggy eyes still followed me. There was no escape. Dear Lord, why didn't someone bury that poor thing??

I would come home crying, and finally begging Dad to not make me go there anymore. He relented, so for a while, I didn't go at all. But, inside, I missed what should have been. All my life, I knew that something was missing. There was an emptiness that gnawed away at the very core of my being.

God is so good. One day, a retired neighbor and his wife stopped by our farm. They invited Dad and Mom to visit their little country church. They also offered to come to our house, pick up my sister and I, and take us to church with them. I rode to church with them for many years. I still remember and treasure them, and that church, how it looked, how it smelled, and everyone who went there. The building is still standing – empty - but standing. Like a lot of people – empty, but still standing.

The pastor was a younger man who preached and taught like no one I had ever heard before. I think I was probably in the second grade, maybe third. When he asked if anyone wanted to ask Jesus to come into their heart, I knew that I did. I was so grateful for the haven of that place. It was the home base for my peace. This was also the home base for finding out that I could nearly levitate my 6' 2", 225 lb. Dad straight off his chair!!! I came home from church one Sunday and told them that when I grew up, I wanted to marry a pastor and have five boys, one girl, and sit in the front row…. That did it!!!! My Dad didn't have the same feelings about serving our Lord as I did.

This church was a blessing to my whole family, and our community. We began to have sliding parties on our big hill for the youth groups in the winter, and bonfire cookouts in the summer. Mom loved them! She would heat 5- gallon cans of milk for homemade hot chocolate while Dad and I would haul loads of dead tree limbs for the fires, and straw bales to sit on. The fires could be seen for miles, and everyone who seen the fire came over. There were many cars parked on the road and in the field. Everyone had a wonderful time roasting hotdogs, marshmallows, sliding, skiing, toboggans, and enjoying the blessings God gave us. In the summer, the kids ran and played, chasing lightning bugs and each other, while the parents relaxed and enjoyed the companionship of neighbors and family.

I look back and see the "wasted" time in my life and the great many mistakes that I have made because even though I had joyfully accepted that Jesus IS my savior, I was never told that I could have a personal relationship with Him. Sadly, most churches don't explain repentance or follow up with those who want to know more.

I started reading the Bible many times from the beginning. That is the logical place to start reading a book. But, when I got to the 'begats', I got discouraged and would quit for a while. I had no one to help me. It was definitely not encouraged at home. I remember Aug. 28, 1968 – the day I paid 75 cents for a Bible of my own. Howled at for hours – actually, off and on for a long time – for wasting precious hard-earned money on something as stupid as a Bible. A Bible is not stupid. It is the only "operation manual" for living a life that works. "Basic Instructions Before Leaving Earth". I still have that precious book. It is so very fragile and falling apart – but praises to our Lord – I am not!!!

In the meantime, life was moving me on. Time does not stand still for anyone. Lessons are learned, mistakes are made. Things happen to us and around us that change who we think we are, and how we think others see us. I truly believe that is the most damaging part. Shame and regret destroy one's self- confidence and hope for the future.

At the end of my fourth-grade year, our little country school closed. They called it 'consolidation'. For me – it was horrible. Now, instead of twenty kids in the whole school, there were over fifty in each grade. And most were unpleasant to country kids in secondhand clothes and no TV. Why did all that matter? I didn't understand it then. I don't understand it now. I did know then, that if one person thinks they are superior- then automatically – someone else must be inferior. I remember lying in bed at night, with "my" baby sleeping peacefully beside me, and praying. I would ask God why they treated me like that…. Lord, why can't they see past this???

It hurt so bad to see their long, thick, shining, beautiful hair and I had none.

Some of them would purposely walk by me just to flip their hair in my face. And laugh. (Keep in mind – these were the beginning of the 'big hair' days…. Hair was glorified and flaunted in every imaginable way…. The roots of 'mousse abuse'!!!) They were so beautiful – so petite, and so blessed. Not once, did I ever wish that this would happen to them. And never once did I ask God, *"Why me?"* I would think *"Why not me???"* If this had to happen – I still - to this day - can't think of anyone I would wish it on. I knew that somehow – somewhere – He would make it all ok. I would lay there and cry and thank Him that they didn't have to go through this.

After one incredibly bad day, I did get to the point where I asked Him if someone could sneak in, in the middle of the night and shave the head of the worst tormentor…. I said, "Lord, it will grow back – but for just a while, she will feel a little bit of what I am going through… Father…. Please forgive me…

But - every black cloud has a silver lining. Sometimes, as Dad always said, we just have to look harder to find it. I made a few lifelong friends and many memories. One of them was a boy on our bus, who for no reason I could ever think of, stood up in a big way for a fat, ugly, barn smelling girl who had to wear a cheap, horrid wig. For a long time, he never even spoke to me. But, if someone pulled the wig off or hurt me, he retaliated. No matter that he was a smaller built young man and sometimes the adversary was very large! He was protective to the point of keeping me from quitting school because I couldn't bear the teasing and bullying anymore. On my bad days, he drove many miles to pick me up and bring me home, so I wouldn't have to ride the bus. And, I recently had the pleasure of telling his beautiful wife how much I still appreciate all the things that he had done for me when we were growing up. I have thanked God for him many times. He also shared my love of fast flying Mopars, to the extent of installing "hood pins" on my gorgeous Coronet 440 when the hood would pop up if I "accidently went slightly airborne…" He was an unbelievable blessing to me and my children for many years.

As my older sister and I were growing up, like all children, our greatest influence was from our parents. Our mother was quiet about most things, we basically had no relationship with her at all. She never told us – even in private - that the things Dad was indelibly stamping in our minds were wrong. I think that her faith was strong, as I look back now, but her ability to stand up to her husband was missing in action – with good reason. She was afraid of angering him and she wasn't a fighter. Since she knew that her opinion didn't count unless it gave credence to Dad's, he had mental free range over us. Plus, I don't think she honestly cared. She just wanted us out of the house.

Now – I truly cannot emphasize this enough – he meant no harm. The things he told us and taught us, he truly believed were the truth and in our best interests. *Always.* The last thing he would ever have wanted was to see us hurt. In his eyes, we were both overweight, and unattractive, and he knew that boys, and men were naturally attracted to the thin, attractive girls and women. He was afraid that we would have to live alone and have no one to care. Please – *always* - keep this in mind. His view of life came from his life observations and experiences –as do ours. My relationship with him was akin to the relationship between "Pa" and "Laura" on the television show "Little House on the Prairie". The huge defining difference was that the "Dad" on the television show believed in and followed the Lord - mine did not. I loved him, honored, and respected him then as I still do today.

Raising a child is the biggest and most important job a person can ever be given. From the second the umbilical cord is cut, by most state's laws, you only have 18 years to raise a responsible, self-supporting, law abiding, and good choice making, honest citizen. A respectful, responsible adult will be an asset to the community and the world – not a liability. The clock is ticking. Don't waste a teachable moment. You may never have the opportunity again. If there is an "Information void" in a child's mind – fill it with Godly values and logical wisdom. Don't let someone else fill it with garbage. We are all the children of God. Therefore, we are all brothers and sisters. We don't all look alike, sound alike, or dress alike. But we are all part of God's family. Be the role model that your children will want to follow. They will have a clearer path as adults because of your example.

We were told "Do as I say. Not as I do." So – what do you think we noticed first???? I recently read that we forget 80% of what we hear but remember 80% of what we see. Be careful little eyes what you see – be careful little ears what you hear. There is no 'delete' key. Our minds and bodies are made by God. Don't desecrate them. Keep them pure, healthy and strong. There is another old saying- "If it isn't in the bottom of the well – it can't come up in the bucket." Think about that. What are you allowing to pollute their well, and yours? Your strong, healthy, clean mind and body is where you live. Where would you be without them?

There were always little signs posted around my Dad's desk. One said, "If you're not part of the solution, you are part of the problem." With our heads filled with impure, inappropriate thoughts, how can we be a solution to anyone's problems? No matter what the world says, there is definitely "right" and "wrong". One helps, one harms. (One year I found a sign for him that says, "You and I have a strange and unique relationship. You're strange, and I'm unique". He laughed until he cried, and I still have the sign! A precious memory!)

Teaching respect for oneself and others is important. I was taught that JOY comes from Jesus, Others, and You. But I was taught from Day 1 that feelings (mine) didn't matter. Attitude does. So, while I can't change what others think of me, I alone can determine how I react to them. A beloved pastor once said to me, "I have never met anyone like you. You fall down the stairs, make sure that everything still works, get up, and say "Thank You Lord! That is over!"

I asked, "What else could I do? God knew it was going to happen, He'll get me through it, and I'm moving on!!" *This too has come to pass.*

*It only comes to stay if I hold on to it. Let it go. There are far better things to hold onto!* "If He leads you to it, He will bring you through it."

I saw myself as a tool. It didn't dawn on me that tools were made to be used. I had been mentally set up to accept that being used and disrespected was normal. When one has a low self-value, the natural reaction from others will reflect that also. No more. Now, I know that I'm God's child. In His loving care. God's truth set me free.

When I was beginning my sophomore year, this wonderful Pastor told Dad and me that I was eligible for a full scholarship into an excellent Bible college, only a couple of hours away. I wouldn't have to worry about tuition, room and board, books, etc., plus a stipend, all through the church. I could have easily and joyfully gone into missions. Dad said, "NO. That is not going to happen." He didn't want one of his kids in any form of ministry anywhere, and he figured that someday, somehow, someone would hit him up for money… Money was his God. The Bible says that "the LOVE of money is the root of all evil…" 1 Timothy 6:10. He feared "being broke" more than eternity in hell and valued his money more than Heaven. Sad. And "being stuck supporting" two unappealing girls was not high on his list. Money IS important, it is how we buy groceries, acquire housing, transportation, healthcare, etc. It is a necessity. Money is a tool. To support yourself, your family, and to help others. God and His children are our reason to live, thrive, and be happily rejoicing in His love and presence. I remember hearing of a rich man who wanted to be buried in a Cadillac and take ALL his money with him.

So…. his wife built a wooden box, found a Cadillac hood ornament at a junk yard, nailed it on, and wrote him a check….

I have always asked God for "enough". Enough to meet my needs and help those He places in my path. Not a lack, so I would think He doesn't care, and not so much that I think I did it myself and don't need Him. JUST ENOUGH.

For some reason, Dad always thought I wasn't the brightest bulb in the box. And I probably wasn't. But… I had NO time to study, to read assignments, and still got mostly A's, and a few B's from listening in class and rapidly scanning highlights from books while riding to and from school, and during a rare study hall. When my sister started high school, she quit going to the barn, so she was able to spend all her time studying. Despite the way my life was, the guidance counselor said that

I had the highest ASVAB (Armed Services Vocational Aptitude Battery exam) score in mechanical ability ever recorded in our school district's history, and very high in law enforcement. But with my abnormal health difficulties, I was ineligible for either field.

*Psychology teaches the nature versus nurture components in childhood development. I believe that they come together in a child's mind from birth. I have always questioned the word 'childhood'. In reality, childhood is the boot camp for life. When we play with dolls, we are practicing our instinctive mothering skills. We play with bulldozers and trucks to learn mechanical and spatial relations. Toys mimic and teach adult skills.*

*I recently listened to a young lady telling how, as from a very small child; she couldn't wait to get a new Barbie doll. She loved to dress them and experiment with different hair styles. She was relating that to me because she felt that it was the beginning of her lifelong passion. She is an excellent hair stylist. We have chores to do in our homes so that when we grow up, we know how to care for ourselves – and the home. We also learn that there are things we can touch – and a lot that we cannot. We are taught boundaries and self-control.*

*In college, we were taught the blank slate theory, and I don't buy that. From birth, every creation has individual needs, desires, and tastes. Each baby is born with a unique foundation from which thoughts, words, and deeds are processed somewhat differently.*

*I look it as my 'motherboard' concept. Every computer has a motherboard. Then, according to the purchase order, software is installed to process specific items. If it is set up to process banking, it won't do well with making menu selections and choosing proper recipes.*

*Each child conceived is an individual miracle. God picks and chooses DNA from ancestors until He gets us exactly right. I picture Him – like a painter carefully picking the right combinations of colors and design until each individual is a perfect masterpiece. Inimitable – irreplaceable! And with an individual purpose and unique abilities.*

*We must be different. Not everyone can be a computer programmer. We need doctors, farmers, teachers, truck drivers, etc. Think about God's infinitely intricate design. There have been uncounted millions of people (and animals, birds, etc…) uniquely created. There has never been a duplicate. Even identical twins are not identical. At first glance- I have had trouble figuring out who is who. But – a few minutes later – they are very different. Each person has been created divinely and totally unique – for a specific purpose. Not a one has ever been a mistake. We are made for a reason and a purpose. We all have gifts and abilities that are ours alone.*

I grew up knowing that my Dad loved me dearly, but that didn't change the fact that to them, I was an unwanted mistake. They "had tried every kind of birth control available at the time. And none of them worked." Well guess what folks… They all worked for eight months… In the ninth month, God made me!!!! I was HIS choice – NOT yours. You were the two specific people He used to bring me to life. When you think about how much your earthly dad loved you, (or God forgive him – didn't….), think of our heavenly Father holding you as a newborn, tears in His eyes, loving you and wanting to provide all that your heart needs and desires. There will NEVER be anyone else exactly like you in the world. Just to go to Him and thank Him for loving you so much and accept His love, guidance, and provision. Thank You, Father God for my life!!!

Physically, I look like my grandmother and her youngest sister, I was very submissive, like my Mother. Giving my life to our Lord set me free from a lot of old earthly chains and ideas. I now am under His guidance. Not my Dad's. And praise God – I inherited some spunk and love of adventure from the amazing women on both sides.

But the gift God planted in me that I am most grateful for is the inheritance of my great aunt's love for the Lord. She would visit every few summers for a week. She would sit quietly on the bed and read the Bible every morning. I would sit silently by the bedroom door and watch her. It brought me great peace. I knew I was in the presence of something special. She knew I was there, would see me, and smile. When she was done reading and praying, sometimes she would read to me. Precious memories…. Never forgotten. Her faith, which I didn't intellectually understand, warmed my heart. I believe that today, all these years later, I am still being blessed by her example and prayers.

As we began to grow out of 'little girlhood', Dad wanted my older sister and me to understand that because we were both "fat and ugly", we couldn't expect the "cream of the crop" of young men to 'come calling'. The "young man – when you go out to woo, think not of who you'll have – but who'll have you." was repeated, gender rearranged for the occasion. And I was not only fat and ugly, but now I was really up the yonder creek without a paddle, because I was totally undesirable - I was a 'blooper'. (Not physically perfect…) He didn't want me to be disappointed. In his way, he was trying to set me up to not expect much from life, therefore – warding off the hurts and pain from rejection. In the only way that he could think of, he tried to shield me from the pain of probable rejection. I was "Daddy's girl", I loved him, I respected him, and I trusted him completely. I believed every word that he said. Unconditionally. Back in his day's mind set, a woman was only as good as who she married. A woman wasn't anything on her own. She took on her husband's identity. At least, that is what we were taught. In his eyes, there was no hope of us "marrying well". This was the basis for his trying to prepare us for what he was sure to be a dismal future. Dad's version of the Beatitudes was "Blessed are those who have low expectations- for they shall not be disappointed." And – he truly did not want us disappointed or hurt.

My older sister and I grew up knowing that as children, we were not seen as gifts from God, but as our recent president stated, a punishment for a mistake. I remember hearing on my fourth birthday "You are four now – fourteen more years and you are out of here." I remember thinking that was too far off to worry about now. And life went on as usual. Every year, it was restated – math updated… When one grows up in an animal-agricultural farm life, your sensitivities are somewhat muted. Beautiful baby calves are born, raised and loved – played with like puppies (they all had names and answered to them), but at the end of the day, you know that one day they will be gone. Beaten, cattle-prodded onto a truck, scared, terrified, lost, and totally betrayed. You could see the tears, fears, and pain in their eyes. "Don't get attached". "It's just an animal." "Get over it." "You are just a big crybaby." So, harden your heart. Don't show your pain. Do your crying in the rain – no one will see. And know that what comes, and you love - will go – just a matter of time. Suck it up and deal with it. But while those precious lives are in your care - love them and treat them the best you can. If God gave me a day to get up and go to the barn, I considered myself blessed. One day at a time. I would worry about tomorrow when it came. This was by no means a firm, unshakable emotional foundation for a stable life. It was totally devoid of hope for a future.

In the summer after fifth grade, I started feeling that I needed to earn some money. I was determined that my beautiful little sister wouldn't have to wear second-hand clothes. I wanted her to have a better life than I had. What I wore didn't matter – my life was already pretty much set at a lower bar. But- she was going to sail over the highest one with room to spare. I got a job cleaning house for an elderly retired teacher. I loved her dearly and called her "Gramma B". She would play the piano and her autoharp for me while I worked. Beautiful old hymns!! When I was asked to sing at a wedding in our church, she practiced with me, loving and supporting me. She was a huge positive influence and inspiration for me. I learned a lot from her that is still valuable today. Every Saturday morning after milking, barn cleaning, and my weekly calf pen cleaning, I would clean up and literally run approximately three miles to her house. I would clean like a hurricane all day. Then, run home to get ready to do the evening chores. Gramma B paid me $1.00/hr., plus lunch. I felt rich! If I ran fast, I could get 6-7 hours in. That would buy books, toys, and clothes for the baby.

It may sound odd – but – I loved my life! I simply cannot ever fathom growing up anywhere else. I would have felt like a dog in a cage, had I been raised in a city. With the advent of the bigger school, came the new friends only a few miles away that we never knew existed! A new girl, two years older than my older sister – loud, outspoken, funny, and always full of life, became one of my best friends ever. And, with only three miles between farms – we could easily walk that after chores! Great summer fun! And there were enough of us then, that if one of us had a lot of hay down, rocks to pick, or other heavy work to be done, someone would come help, or at least cheer us on!

There were plenty of country kid mischief and shenanigans.... Like accidentally dumping a five-gallon bucket of ice cold well water out the haymow door onto Dad's head, instead of the intended target of my older sister.... And how we ever got it up there is another story by itself... My best friend Tessa and I camped out in the haymow for a few nights while my poor Daddy regained his sense of humor... There was always another episode at "camp run amuck" that left Dad laughing so hard that he could hardly stand up, and Mom screaming her head off at all three of us.

One of those moments occurred one spring morning, when the barnyard was full of soft squishy "cow poo", and the ground was still too wet to get the tractor in there to clean it out. Because of the unusual barnyard condition, Tessa and I had been getting on our favorite big Brown Swiss cow, riding her out of the barn and disembarking on higher, dryer ground. We would climb up and get on her back and open her stanchion with our toes. It worked very well until one day when I said something stupid, and Tessa shoved me off and I landed in the mess. On my backside... up to my armpits! So... I reached down and found a small rock and threw it at Melody. She jumped sideways and Tessa landed right beside me in the stinky mess! We instantly heard Dad laughing so hard that he could barely stand up! He had to hang onto the wooden gate to try to catch his breath! All the while Mom was screaming his name and yelling about us... "do something with them!!! Do you see what they just did??? Do something!" over and over and over and over...... and every time she yelled, he laughed harder. And poor Melody didn't know what to think. She wanted to come back to get us, but not with Mom screeching... And she knew that they should be heading up to the forty, but she wouldn't go without us.

Finally, Dad was able to catch his breath and say, "It's all ok. Go get them clean clothes and they can shower and clean up in the milkhouse!" So, after a few more death-defying glares, she took his advice, and he took the cows up to pasture while we cleaned up. Dad laughed about that every time he thought about it for the rest of his life, and Mom still growled and grumbled. "The more things change, the more they stay the same...."

And, then there was a young man who had my heart from the beginning. Much taller, larger, quieter, more gentle and patient than any person I had ever met – I finally felt safe and secure when I was with him. We built a strong friendship. Of course, the teasing ensued. We ignored it and enjoyed each other's company. I remember about a year after we met, he was drug by a heifer in the barn and taken to the local hospital. I rode into town with Dad when he went to get feed and spent the day there with him. I had to know that he would be ok. He recovered, and life moved on. All our schoolmates and our community assumed that we would be a lifetime thing.

The years of schooling from fifth to senior seemed to fly by. I grew into more responsibility with the farm and 'my' baby was growing beautifully. I was busy with raising a child, farming, babysitting for neighbors 3-4 nights a week, and cleaning house. One year melted into the next. Somewhere around the end of her eighth-grade year, my older sister began to date a much older man. He was a good choice for her, according to Dad. He could afford to support a wife, and if she wanted to go to college – it would be their issue. She too, had learned most of the same life lessons that I had. Hers were tempered somewhat by loving and supportive grandparents. From that time on, she was relieved from much of the outside work. She was highly encouraged to get as much education as possible. Study hard. Get good grades. She was smart… and I wasn't – according to our parents. ("She got the brains, the little one got the looks, but Mya in the middle got left out – poor thing. But she has a good attitude, and she tries hard….") Mom always said, "Mya was made to work, they were made to be pretty." That works for me, it's much easier to work than to maintain "pretty" …..

I was grateful for what I had. Dad only let me take Home Economics, where I was blessed with one of the best teachers ever, and general math. "There was no possibility" that I would ever "amount to anything", so I wasn't allowed to take typing, bookkeeping, biology, chemistry, algebra, etc. And – "You already know how to heat bottles, change diapers, cook, clean house, and milk cows." We both knew that our lives were going to take different courses. She knew what she was going to do. And I thought that I did. She still helped some in the summer with the haying and in the barn when required. She didn't mind driving the tractors. Picture me trying to load bales on a hay wagon – and keep them on while she is driving like she's on a horse doing a barrel race at the rodeo… Oh, good times!!! She would laugh her head off when the outside tier would fall off and I'd have to reload it all. Dad's bales averaged 80-100 pounds. They were stacked 3-4 rows high plus 2 "binder rows" on top of them to hold them on. In 80–90-degree heat. And we have beautiful rolling hills…. I would have to reload almost every load…

One day, Dad sent me down to Gramma B's with the narrow front-end tractor to rake the hay so we could bale it. I wasn't feeling up to par, but I went anyway. When I was just about done, I turned too short. The rake caught on the lugs of the big tractor tire, and the rake was thrown up, and almost hit me. I rapidly stopped, got off, and walked to Gramma B's house. I told her what happened, called Dad and told him which tractor to bring, and he came. He lifted the rake down of the tire and asked me if I wanted to finish raking or go home and do the chores. I said, "I'll go milk the cows and do the chores.…" We got done about the same time, and on the way to the house I asked him if I could take the car to town. He said, "Sure." So, I showered and headed to the emergency room. My doctor who delivered me was on call. My temperature was a wee bit over 104. I had tonsillitis and was given antibiotics. Went home. Went to bed. Got up in the morning. Milked the cows. Baled the hay. Life went on.…

Dad had built a platform on the back of the row crop Case tractor. The platform could raise up on the hydraulic arms if necessary. It was used to pick up newborn calves in the pasture and carry them home, so they didn't have to walk. Momma could walk beside them and supervise their transport. Well…. One day, when I was sitting on this platform, holding a brand-new baby calf, my dear sister decided to see how fast she could pivot the tractor before both the calf, and I set sail. Thankfully, by the grace of God neither of us were hurt. I was not amused.

It seemed like we blinked twice and found ourselves planning her graduation and wedding. I would ask her periodically if she was happy. We had become very efficient at squeezing the lemons that life handed to us and making the best lemonade possible. The trouble was, and still is, neither of us like lemonade.… I assumed she was happy, but, sometimes, I could see sadness underneath.

I read somewhere a few years ago that a surprisingly large percentage of women have great uncertainty about going through with their weddings. I have seen that. I have watched it up close and personal - many times.

But, being "sturdy Swedes", we went on. We didn't see any other choices. We knew that once we turned eighteen, we were out the door. We had never held a job in town because our time was spent working the farm or doing schoolwork. As a result, we had no "job experience" with "transferable skills".

Years later, we were talking about this period in our lives. She said that people make decisions with the information that they have at that moment, and with the options that they can see. If they had more information – or had seen better options – they would have made a different decision. Very simple. Very true. Many years later, someone gave more enlightenment on decision making. He said to first determine if it is a 'reversible' decision or an 'irreversible' decision. For example – selling a house…. (Odds are good that you can't get it back), putting a pet to sleep, etc. On the other hand, if you paint the living room purple, it can be re-painted. Evaluate the potential costs of the "reversal", financially, physically, emotionally, and mentally when you try to discern the decisions that may be reversible at a greater expense… It was great advice that I will not forget.

I was so proud of my older sister when she graduated – she made Valedictorian. A great honor for a lot of hard work. This was followed by a house full of white satin, lace, thread balls, and stitch rippers. She had decided to create her own wedding dress. A couple of cheap fabric "dry runs", viola – a gorgeous gown! Smart – and creative. And very determined. All the secrets of success nailed firmly down! I watched this and cheered as I ran in and out of the house busy with the summer field work.

My big teddy bear would bring me a box of chocolate covered cherries on every Saturday night date, and while I liked one or two – they were mostly fuel for wedding dress creation, they didn't go to waste! The wedding was what Dad called "the social event of the season" in the neighborhood. It was beautiful and over so quickly. She had moved out. Dad said, "One down – one to go…"

With her gone, things seemed ominous for me. I kept going to church, missed her singing with me, going for walks, and just knowing that she was there. She was in an apartment in town, about ten miles away. But for me there was an eerie – 'now what' – feeling. It was a field marker- a 10-yard line. But – no touch down in sight. So, I kept busy. Hard work is a great thing. An occupied mind doesn't have time to fear.

A tired body sleeps well at night. And there is a sense of accomplishment in a job well done. Dad used to ask us "If you don't have time to do it right the first time, when are you going have the time to do it over?????" Good point. Never forgotten. I worked hard that summer and prepared for my first year in school without my older sister. Not that we spent much time together – but, it had helped just knowing that she was there.

I had struggled on an aunt's hard-boiled egg diet all summer to get ready for the wedding, so I wasn't quite as fat. Somehow, I thought that might make me more socially acceptable. Mom had sewn a dress for me out of the leftover practice material. It was the first "new" dress that I'd ever had. *Father God, please get me through this somehow......*

Well- God in His infinite wisdom, mercy, great sense of humor, and love – had given me a "Dukes of Hazard" love of all things with large powerful engines, and loud, rumbling – back then- glass pack exhaust systems!!! I was raised by a man who let me help tear down the 53 Studebaker Hawk when I was about six, get the valves ground, and help put it back together. And… it ran beautifully!

I grew up driving tractors, the 1966 International farm truck; knowing how to gap spark plugs, their firing orders, changing oil and filters, hunting up grease fittings, changing tires, etc. He rocked my whole world when he came home with a jet black 1963 Plymouth Fury III. It had a 361 big block, 3 on the tree – unsynchronized low (which I figured out how to downshift without coming to a complete stop – much to his dismay!!!) 65 – Drop her into second – rocket on to 95 – drop her into high – or foul out a plug. I gapped and changed one plug. Never again. Changing a plug in the pouring down rain in the middle of a cold October night was not my idea of a good time.

He also taught me about cornering – rear wheel drive only. (I have no idea about front wheel drives. And I am too old to learn!) "For Pete's sake – slow down a little bit before you hit the corner Mya. But – if you can't slow it down enough – halfway through the corner – hit the gas hard enough to break it loose (controlled fishtail), and it will correct itself" Thank you Dad…. That worked beautifully!! And – way more fun than just slowing down.

I remember coming home late for chores one day. I thought Dad would be safely in the barn – along with all the neighboring potential witnesses…. Well, he just happened to be coming out of the barn – heading for the milkhouse in time to see me shooting past the driveway…. Ohhhh boy… I pulled into the garage, got out, and was met by a screaming irate Dad…. "What in the world…. did you think you were doing when you went past the driveway???????" I looked at him calmly and said, "95. That is why I didn't stop. I couldn't. I had to go up to the corner, turn around and come back." All true. Never lie to your parents. Then – Praise God!!! He started to laugh until I thought he was going to choke! "It's my own fault – that's what I taught you and you learned it well!" Oh yes - I did.

A few years later, I was thinking about buying that car from him. An older friend asked me, "How are you going to be able to afford that thing? Gas might go up to fifty cents a gallon!!!" To this day, I wish I had bought it…

We were in another town later that summer, getting farm supplies, about forty miles away when we went by a Dodge dealership. I spotted a Dodge Super Bee. I just about jumped out the window! I had to drive that! Dad said "OK." I pulled in and asked if I could drive it. The salesman asked if we wanted him to ride with…. I politely said, "No sir. I don't." So, with Dad in the passenger seat, I put one foot on the brake, one on the clutch, and turned on the key to the most amazing rumbling roar that I had ever heard! Every cell in my body was on high alert! At the same time, I popped the clutch and hit the gas! That magical piece of automotive mania walked around in a tight circle. I looked, and we were exactly where we started out from. Except that we had a large audience – laughing and clapping!! That is when I discovered what a "racing rear-end" was. I tried it again – a wee bit slower - and went for a very exhilarating ride. One more crazy car story and I promise I will move on…

When I got my driver's license, sometimes Dad let me drive the 'big Plymouth' to school when I had to help finish the morning milking. I didn't have to be subjected to the tortures of the bus, and I could get more done before I had to leave. The bus came at 7:30 a.m. and I didn't have to leave that early if I drove. So…. One morning he got a call from our high school principal. This was the same man who complained about my being late frequently because Mom was sick and couldn't help with the barn chores.

One day when he called, Dad told him that he had worked out a great solution to that problem. Mr. Principal asked what that would be… Dad said, "Well. If you come help me in the barn, she can get to school on time." Never had another call on that subject… But there always seemed to be more subjects…….

"Well, Mr., do you have any idea what your daughter is doing now???" Dad said, "Uhhh…. No, I'm here, and she isn't. Pray tell… What is she doing?" "Well… Donuts. She's out in the faculty parking lot doing donuts!" (It was winter, and the lot was covered in beautifully icy hard packed snow!!! Couldn't let that go to waste…) My Dad quietly asked, "Has she hit anything yet?" "No." Dad said, "Well, call me back when she does!" Click. He never received a return call. There was no sign stating that it was not to be done, and since students parked on one end…. Looking back at my life, I seriously see countless times God has protected me from me!!!

All through my junior year, I was given more responsibility at home, and more encouragement to 'go out and have some fun' by my dad. The kind of 'fun' he had not been allowed to have. We didn't drink, smoke, do drugs, etc. What I didn't realize was that he was trying to separate me from my 'silly attachment' to someone he seen as an 'undesirable' young man. Dad admired men who dressed 'fancy', drove fast, expensive cars, and 'dated' beautiful thin women – whether they were married or not. He idolized J.R. Ewing. My calm, heavy-set, peaceful teddy bear didn't fit any of his specifications as a suitable father for future grandchildren.

There was a young man who would call Dad and ask him if I could go out with him. And Dad thought it was a good idea. "He's a really nice guy". I always told Dad, "If you think he's such a really nice guy, then you go with him. I'm going to go clean the chicken coop." Or calf pens, or whatever was the most pressing. And way more enjoyable than that….

I was too naive and trusting to see through any of his manipulations. So, highly encouraged in the wrong direction, I made mistakes. And, they were applauded by my dad. Inside, I felt dirtier and more defiled. I could see no way out. Either way, I would disappoint Dad or me. Most times – I disappointed me. I could not disappoint Dad. I wanted his approval, and his love. And my mother never said one word.

People see what we do…. But God knows why we did it. He knows our hearts. I never knew that my Heavenly Father would lead me and guide me to the right path. I didn't know that I could ask. How could our perfect, Holy amazing Father even stand to look down at me? I was convinced that He could never love a broken mess – a substandard, imperfect, hopeless mess like me. No one had ever told me about His loving forgiveness. To me, my life was permanently stained with shame and regret. And there was no way out.

Always in the back of my mind – 18 – was coming closer - like a roaring freight train. And I was still stalled on the tracks.

In the spring of that year, my grandparents planned a trip to visit Grandpa's brother in Ohio. They had always taken my older sister on their annual treks. But, this year, she was married. Someone suggested to them, that it would be the right thing to invite me. So, after much discussion, I was asked. Hoping that this would bring me closer to them, I went. Before we left, I knew, and told a couple close friends, that we would be in a car accident. We left early in May for what was intended to be a two-week vacation. I took all my books and homework with me. My grandmother was always very thin and had stomach problems. It was hard to watch her struggle. I tried to understand what was wrong, because I had the same health issues that I had seen in her. We were both seriously anemic, had bleeding ulcers, and low blood sugar issues. I would try to talk to her, but she would just turn her head away in silence. This road trip would be very difficult for her. (Years later, I mentioned this at a family gathering. No one else had ever noticed. Father, please help us to be more observant and helpful to others.) We safely arrived, and I met my great uncle for the first time. He was a very quiet and respectful gentleman. I was greatly impressed with him – his manners, countenance, dignity, and intelligence. I was blessed to have had the privilege of meeting him. We stayed for a week, repacked and left for home.

We drove for a while and stopped for gas. When we pulled out of the station, I remember Grandpa saying that the hill we were going to go down was very steep. From the back seat, I couldn't see over the long hood of the 1967 Ford Galaxy 500. I thank God for that hood, and the rock-solid steel frame. My Grandfather didn't trust the brakes to hold the car on a hill that steep, so he down shifted the automatic transmission into 'Drive 2'. I remember getting safely to the bottom of the hill, and a stop sign. It was a strange, blind corner with a railroad trestle blocking the view. We all looked and didn't see anything coming, and he hit the gas. That was the last thing I remember.

Unbeknownst to us, we had been hit by a 21-ton loaded coal truck at a relatively high speed. The bystanders made an emergency call and told them that not to hurry, because we were all dead. So, when ambulances did arrive – they were surprised to find three living people. All out cold, but alive. That big, solid Ford's whole front end was trashed. Gone. Pieces scattered all over. But both doors still opened!!!! It was a two door, so fishing me out of the back seat was quite a project. I think it involved the Jaws of Life. None of us remembered anything after stopping at that light. I have thanked Him for that. The first thing I do remember was several days later. My Dad and older sister had jumped into the fast, flying Fury and headed to Ohio. Since my sister also knew what an accelerator pedal was for, they arrived in record time. Her thoughtfulness included a stop at a store and picking up a rather expensive - $58.00 - and gorgeous wig for me. Mine was ruined. For the first time – ever – I didn't completely feel like a freak while wearing one!!! Dad always said, "Every cloud has a silver lining. Sometimes we just have to look harder…." This was a silver lining moment!

Then finally came the moment that I could hear Dad's voice. He was out at the nurses' station speaking loudly and forcefully at them! I am pretty sure that every conscious - or not - person on that floor heard him. "Why isn't she awake??? What are you doing to get her to come to???" All the way to "What are you going to feed her when she does come to???" I heard the poor nurse saying that I would be on a liquid diet… Beef broth, Jell-O, and tea. He said, "There is no way she will wake up for that!!! She will never eat that!!!"

He was partly right - I wouldn't have eaten that, but I would awaken. I kept trying to say, "Dad…. Calm down. I am ok. I feel like I am in a glass box and can't get out…… Peace- be still - and give me a little more time to figure this one out!!!" He couldn't hear me, but I could hear everything. My sister spent her time going back and forth between her beloved grandparent's rooms, loving and comforting them. They and my uncle all felt that it was their fault that I was in this coma for five days. It was no one's fault. Nothing ever happens that makes God go – "Oh no…. I never thought about that…. Now what…. ". That's what we do – not Him!! A few more days and I finally came to. I looked at Dad and asked about my grandparents. I wasn't allowed to see them… I never did understand that.

My legs had been badly crushed, battered, and bruised. There were cuts and stitches where the doctors had to dig parts of the battery out, amongst other things. There were dents in my skull and traumatic brain injuries from the impact. I guess being a "hard-headed Swede" helped! When I was released, I could barely walk enough to get in and out of the car. I don't remember much about the ride home. I went in and out of awareness of my surroundings.

When we finally got home, I was faced with new problems. I couldn't walk or see well. My glasses had been smashed, my head injuries affected my vision and migraine headaches began. My legs were in agony. Charlie horses were so intense that I could only scream with the excruciating pain. Nights were the worst, all night for months. Nothing helped. My doctor said that veins and cells had been damaged or crushed, so now the blood had to find new pathways that weren't blocked.

My books and homework had been destroyed, along with everything else, in the impact. So, now, a few days before the end of the school year, without my friends, I would have been sunk. The principal, who had been head-to-head with us for a long time, also taught one of my classes. All the other teachers said they would average the grades that I had before I left. Not this one. He wanted everything turned in. He wanted recompense. It mattered not that I had a solid A before the accident. No mercy – no grace. But praises to God – there were three friends who came over and got all the required work done for me. He couldn't fail me, but I did receive a "D-". Oh well…. It was over. It took a while before my eyes could be retested and new glasses ordered. I missed my cousin's graduation. I missed everything for a while… But I was still alive. And I started walking again with less pain!!! Praises to God!

My grandparents' condition was much worse. Being in the front seat, they had borne the brunt of the impact. My beautiful, fragile Grandmother had many broken bones in all parts of her body. She was in the hospital until around Christmas when an ambulance brought her to a local nursing home for the rest of her life.

I was blessed to be able to go visit her, and when she could no longer hold a spoon to eat by herself, I got up two hours earlier, drove to her, fed her and was still able to get the kids to school; and make it to work on time. And drove back to feed her supper. I was there with her the day she spoke her last words. I told her that I loved her and asked her if she wanted a cup of coffee. She weakly smiled and whispered "yes". Then she absolutely broke my heart. With tear filled eyes, she apologized for how she treated me all my life. And asked for my forgiveness. I hugged her gently and said that it was ok. She softly smiled, held my hand and went into a comatose state. And never woke up.

She had always been my role model. To this day, I can still see her picking up "kindling sticks" for her beautiful wood burning kitchen stove. And watching her brush her beautiful long hair before pinning it up in a bun. She saved the hair from the brush and put it on the lilac bush "because the birds use it for soft lining in their nests". She moisturized her skin with fresh cream, skimmed off the top of the milk. She had less wrinkles when she passed away in her 90's, than most 40-year-old ladies do. Her donut recipe is still alive and well in my family, as are many others. I learned so many things from just watching her from a distance. A major one is when she told "a nosy neighbor" that "it seems to me that if I spend more time sweeping my own porch, I have less time to worry about the crumbs on someone else's steps…" You go Gramma!

Grandpa had come home in June. Dad and Mom drove out to get him. He had a follow up appointment at the local hospital soon after coming home. There, a blood clot was discovered in his brain. Since Mom and Dad were gone back to Ohio to visit Gramma, at seventeen, I gave his doctor permission for the necessary surgery and the transfer to a larger specialty hospital. But long- term damage had already been done. His memory was severely damaged. I was his primary care giver while he lived with us, and he followed me closely. He too apologized for the way he treated me all my life. He said that I was worth more than he could see "back then". I told him that it was ok. I loved him and appreciated his example. He still wanted to come help me in the barn but was forgetful and could wander off. He had to be watched closely.

One morning, I had to be in a nearby town to take the college entrance exam. Dad and Mom were still gone, and Grampa couldn't be left alone. Plus, I had a cow close to giving birth, and was running out of options.

Praises to God, He had moved in new neighbors a few years earlier, and one of his sons was the absolute best big brother any girl could ever have! This guy was about five years older than me and extremely protective. There had been a roller-skating date night party that involved all the high school kids in the area. He stopped by that night to talk to Dad about some farm related things and seen me. He said, "Why aren't you at the skating rink? Everyone else is there!" I said, "It's no big deal…" Things clicked in his head as he realized that no one had asked me to go. I had no "date". He got an odd look on his face, looked at me and said, "Go get ready." To Dad he said," We'll pick this up again tomorrow." He looked at me and said, "I'll be back in half an hour, and you'd better be ready." I looked at Dad, and he said, "Go do what he said." So, I did. And when he came back, he was ready to knock the socks off anyone! Wow! "Boy!! Do you clean up good!!!" And, he said, "You look great too, let's go." And we did! When we walked in, he treated me like I was Princess Diana! He skated only with me – even though many beautiful girls were flirting with him. He knew I wasn't the world's best skater because we didn't often go, so I had very little experience. He held on to me, so it looked like I was pretty good. The most amazing night of my life so far!

When back in school on Monday, all the girls wanted to know who he was, and could they have his phone number. I just smiled, and thanked God for him. For the first time in my life, I felt like I wasn't a freak to be laughed at and made fun of. A night to remember.

Back to my current situation with Grampa, I called my "big brother". I told him the dilemma and he responded with, "I'll be there in ten minutes. Get ready to go and I'll take care of it." "Thank you so much!!!" And he was there in exactly ten minutes! I flew the truck into town, ran, and slid into the first available chair. The instructor glared at me, and I smiled back at him and wondered what he'd think if he had had my morning…. I got through it in record time and came out with one of the highest overall scores in our high school. I received offers for fully paid scholarships from several colleges. One was a private school near an Army base where one of my lifelong girlfriend's husband was stationed. They pleaded with Dad to let me go. They would transport me back and forth, and they came home every other weekend. They were close enough that if I had a problem, they could be there quickly. He said, "No." And I again listened to my Dad. I couldn't go against his wishes.

"Meanwhile back at the ranch…." I continued to take care of Grampa as long as I could and carried on. When I had to move out of the house, he was there for a little while until Mom and Dad got tired of taking care of him. I visited him and Gramma as often as I could. He passed away a few years later in a nursing home from pneumonia.

The summer moved into fall, and I was back up and running. I didn't realize that I had any mental residual effects from the accident, until Dad and Mom took my little sister and I school clothes shopping in Minneapolis. There were better thrift stores there... I was ok until a car ran a stoplight, and I started screaming! It stopped within a foot of T-boning us. My first flashback.... It was a long time until I went back into traffic, and no one wanted me to.

My senior year started off unremarkably. Senior pictures, listening to all my classmates excitedly talking about college or marriage. When asked, "What are you going to do?" I had no idea. Show no fear. Walk on. I had applied for college and was accepted. But – no money. Dad wouldn't help. I couldn't get any financial aid unless he would fill out the papers. And he wouldn't. No one had put him through college, he didn't even graduate from high school, and he did ok. (Well – then – can I please farm with you like you did with your Dad??? NO.")

You have no idea how fast September, October, and November can fly by when you know that you will turn the big eighteen in December, and you can't support yourself and still go to high school. "My baby" was now eight, and well-grounded in who she was and still more grounded in who she was not. I raised her to be a strong, discerning little lady. So, if I had to move out, I would miss her, and keep a close eye on her, but I knew she would be ok. One night, I was in bed upstairs, right over the floor register, I heard Dad - out of the clear blue – say, "What in the world are we going to do???" Mom said, "About what?" He said, "Mya. We can't throw her out!!! She hasn't graduated yet. What would the neighbors think???? "

They discussed this more quietly for a while. They decided to have me pay rent. Well, I had been babysitting for several families, after chores and homework, so I figured I could work harder and make it. Pick up a few more weekend things – all is well. $25.00 a week and I had to buy all my own groceries, toilet tissue, clothes, laundry soap, etc. If I wanted it, needed it, or used it or ate it – I bought it. I had my own space in the refrigerator. I couldn't eat anything that wasn't mine. I was ok with that. I was simply thankful for what I had. A roof over my head. I still did morning and evening milking. I still did spring planting- which always involved driving tractors all night (sometimes Tessa drove one too or rode on the fender to keep me awake), haying, fieldwork and feeding, the same as always. I actually did almost all the milking because Dad's knees were getting bad. So, I gave them a break, and they healed and strengthened. Praise God! I milked cows the night that I graduated! Showered, changed clothes, - and flew the Fury into town! I have a picture of me holding my graduation cake and trying to hold back the tears. I knew that whatever little safety and security I did have was gone. Like the last snow in a warm spring rain.

Soon after graduation, I was out in the barn, milking, doing chores as usual.

But I was extremely happy. I had a date with my teddy bear. We had recently looked at a neighboring farm. He said that his parents would 'help us with it when the time came.' At one point, I saw Mom look at Dad in an odd way and then leave the barn. I thought nothing of it. She had to use the bathroom. Nothing unusual. A little while later, she came back. She looked at Dad in the same odd way. This time, he slightly nodded his head. She looked a little nervous as she came towards me. She said that she had some bad news for me. "While I was in the house, his mother had called and said that our date had been canceled. He had found a beautiful, thin girl who had long, thick pretty hair. He never wanted to see me again as long as he lived. I was to never call him again. Ever." Mom and Dad were so sorry. "But – you know – it was bound to happen…. You know how boys are… They like the itty-bitty pretty ones…. With long flowing hair…. You're young. You'll find someone more appropriate…" *More appropriate?? Are you kidding?? What does that mean??? Ok. Breathe deep… suck it up…* I wasn't surprised…. Devastated…Heartbroken… But not surprised. I didn't expect that anyone decent would ever love me. That happened to other girls. Not me. So, I went out with anyone who would ask. At least, I was out of the house and had someone to talk to. If they were happy, at least someone was. But it sure wasn't me. I just wanted someone to love me, value me, need me, and tell me that everything would be ok. I was hollow. Empty. Like a chocolate Easter rabbit. I kept telling myself that it would be ok. I kept the pain and fear from everyone. There was no one to care. Now – I had no one.

Seventeen years later, he and I were talking, and he asked me why I "dumped" him when things were going so well. I stared at him and started crying. "How can *YOU* ask me that when *YOU* didn't have the courage or decency to tell me face to face that you had found your dream girl??? Why??"

He stared at me dumbfounded as I emotionally replayed the whole hurtful thing to him. Then he quietly said, trying to hold back his own tears "I want you to think about something. We had a telephone in the barn. We were all there when *YOUR* mother called *MY* mother. We all saw Mom's face and her tears as she said the words that would tear my heart out – and theirs." He asked me to write a book. He said that I had a story that needed to be told. Sadly a few months later, this amazing man lost his life.

Fall came, and my older sister and I moved about eighty miles away to attend college. I had saved a small amount of money. I paid the first semester's tuition and half of the expenses for our apartment. She was entering her junior year, having completed her associate degree locally. I was going from super small town, USA to huge college life. I was lost and overwhelmed. I hadn't been allowed to take most of the college foundation classes that now were badly needed – like typing!!! And now – I was flat broke. I tried to get a job, but, with no experience in anything and a huge college population, the competition was tough. I was so scared that I called my Dad. He said, "You better figure out something. You are not coming home. There are all sorts of massage parlors there. Have you thought about that?" I said, "NOOOO.... Do you know what they do there????" He said, "Well, you aren't much good at anything else, you might like that!" And he laughed. I loved him unconditionally, and never questioned his instructions. But I couldn't do that.

I had to quit school while I could still get a partial tuition refund. Otherwise, I would be homeless. I went back to our little town and got a job at the grocery store with some help from a friend - and – the grace of God! I worked 45 hours a week and received $45.00 for my work. I waited tables at the local country music bar on band nights and rented a house for $45.00 a month. About a year later, I went to work for a larger company, and worked 54 hours a week for $450.00 a month. I was ecstatic!

One chilly night, I stopped to grab a cup of coffee on the way home from work. Sitting at the counter, was a man who owned a farm several miles away. I had never met him – just heard my friends' older sisters mention him. He had been a senior when I was in third grade. He began to talk to me. He seemed friendly and I thought he looked lonely. So, I stopped and talked to him for a few minutes. He asked me if I liked to bowl. I said that I hadn't had much spare time to go bowling. So, he asked me to go with him. He was lonely, and I had nothing else to do, so we set a time. I didn't tell Dad at all. I didn't want his opinion. This was at the end of November. We went out a couple times. By then, I realized that he was only going out with me because he couldn't find anyone else. One day, I came home from work and heard from my Dad. "I had company today. He said that you two have been dating. And he wanted to know if you had a pendant watch. I was thinking *"Why???"* Then I correctly guessed a Christmas gift. We went out another time, and I came home to meet Dad face to face at the door. I had lost my rental by this time. It had been sold. I had nowhere else to go. So, Mom said that I could come back home for a little while - just until I could find something else.

This man had stopped by to ask Dad if he could marry me, and Dad was delighted. He told me I had to say "Yes". All I heard was a stanchion slamming closed around my neck. *Breathe deep. You can do this. It will be ok. You can make it work. Keep walking.*

"He owns a farm. Four hundred acres of bottom ground!!!" In the spring, I discovered that was true. A lot of it was swamp. "This is the best I'm going to get for you......" Like a cow on the auction block.... And so, I did what Dad told me to do, knowing full well that I was not loved. But I tried.

The date was set – much to the dismay of the whole neighborhood. My Godparents begged my Dad not to make me marry him. They told me I could live with them, as did Grandma B. But I went on. I didn't want to disappoint Dad or this man. I thought that with time, maybe he would come to love me, and that I could make it work. God would work it out. I didn't know that I could ask God what I should do and that He would answer me. I just didn't know… and no one ever told me.

He didn't want to get married in a church. He said that he didn't believe in God. He wouldn't buy a wedding ring for me. He said that IF I was a good wife, he would buy one for me on our fifth anniversary. With no other options, I borrowed Mom's ring for the ceremony. Looking back, I am thankful that I didn't follow my gut instinct and run like a rabbit. I have been blessed with the best children any woman has ever had.

The day before the January wedding, we had a horrid rain. Never heard of before in January, that far north. The barometer dropped to break all records. Then, it froze hard. The wedding morning brought a groom whose truck wouldn't start. He called and told me that I needed to come get him. So, I did. When we arrived at the church, we couldn't get into the parking lot. Neither could the bakery, the florist, or anyone else. Ohhh.... God was sending signs.... But I didn't see them. I didn't know how to hear Him. I had spent my entire life listening to and blindly obeying my Dad and not knowing how to follow God. This was how my life had been so far – why would it be any different now?

We finally got into the church. The furnace had stopped. It was about 55 degrees in there and dropping like a rock. *Ok, Lord.... What's next???* I felt the same trepidation that I had felt a few years earlier. Dad had a firm grasp on my arm as he led me, scared, shaking like a leaf, fighting to hold back tears, up to the altar. Vows, a few pictures, cake, and then worsening weather made for a hasty departure. My sister asked him what she should do with the gifts. "We can't leave them at the church." He said, "Do whatever you want. I don't want them. I don't need them. I have a houseful and I don't want any more stuff." So, I said, "Honey, what if we bring them home and put them in the attic?" He said, "I don't care what they do with them. We are leaving. Let's go. We have cows to milk." The blizzard was raging. Almost everyone else had already left. My older sister and a few close friends and relatives were still there helping to pack up the gifts. I was trying to help clean and straighten up my beloved church for the Sunday service.

We waded out through knee high snow, with drifts forming everywhere. My car started right away. *Thank You Lord.* And we managed to follow the previous set of tracks out of the parking lot. We had only gone a few miles when the car stopped. Ohhh noooo.... I looked at him and said, "Now what..." He said, "It's your car. I guess you better start walking." I quietly said that all I had on were thin dress pants and coat. He said, "Then we'll sit here. I am not walking anywhere." So, I got out in the 30 below zero temperature with a raging wind and walked to the first house, which was nearly a quarter of a mile away. No one was home. I walked on to the next one. I was frozen. A sweet elderly gentleman opened the door and asked, "Can I help you?"

I said "It's too late to help me now. But may I please use your phone?" I called the church, and one of his brothers and my brother-in-law came and jumped the car. We safely made it to my new "home". This was not a good start for a happily ever after. Three days later, after the morning chores, I asked him if I could buy a new pair of 'barn pants' the next time we went to the farm supply store. He asked what size I wore. I told him, and he made a 'disgusted' face, and said, "What??? So and so down the road wears a size 3." So, I asked him, "Well then - why didn't you marry her – oh wait.... Let's see... She is younger than I am. I used to babysit her." That one hurt. Dad's words "Blessed are they who have low expectations – for they will not be disappointed" were flashing back.

Five days later, he ended up in the hospital with an appendicitis. I had taken him to the emergency room, and he was admitted. I had a larger herd of unfamiliar cows and a whole different milking and feeding system than anything I had ever seen. Machines and tractors that were night and day from what I had grown up with. One of his brothers and a nephew came to help a couple of times and then I was on my own. The barn had to be cleaned with a shovel and a wheelbarrow. All 100 feet of it. And there were gutters and large calf pens on both sides. Double the fun on this one! During this time, my mother stopped by. She looked tense and concerned. I asked her what was wrong. It turned out that they had a call from the county clerk. Because of the blizzard, no one had remembered to sign the marriage license. We were not legally married. PRAISE GOD!!!! Hallelujah!!!! I was numb. I was free to go???? And – a big Texas Yee Haw! I am so out of here. But no. Dad had severely lectured Mother that she had to get me into town to sign it. I couldn't let her suffer for my problems. So, she let my younger sister come to stay with me so that I had a friendly face in that spooky old house. A few days later he was released. He was unable to help, but I was grateful that he was home.

He went to his follow up appointments and was healing very well. He still wasn't released to milk, lift, push, or pull. So.... One beautiful cold, crisp morning, I came in from all the barn chores to find his friend there, and him in his snowmobile suit. "What are you doing????" I asked. "What do you think I'm doing?? You aren't that stupid!" was his answer... Guess I was! He tore all the healed tissue apart and needed more stitches.... Another much longer healing process.... I made the best, well kneaded bread in the history of the world that day....

Finally – it was spring! And I was going to be a mother! I was happier than I ever believed possible. It never occurred to me that he wouldn't share my never-ending joy. He was the youngest of a very large family and had many nieces and nephews older than he was. Where I grew up, men didn't often change diapers, heat bottles, feed babies, or do much of anything with children under 5 years old. I assumed that this is how all men were. It didn't stop me from purely rejoicing! I was happy and shared my joy with the whole world! Never mind that I had 'morning' sickness 24-7, the smell of any food would send me running, and the house was full of family all summer. Twenty some people stayed most days and only one bathroom. Mom would come and get me when I was done with chores occasionally so that I had some peace - and no long line for the bathroom. I still drove the tractor on the hay baler, still milked, and still cleaned the barn. I tried to be chef and gracious hostess in my spare time. I was in love with life – no matter what happened. No one could steal my joy.

The cows that he had, were not producing much milk. The July milk check was $98.00. Sadly, it was the same amount as that month's electric bill. That left nothing but my meager savings to pay for other bills, groceries, and grain for the cows. A day or two after receiving the bill, I had to go to Dad and Mom's. As I drove in, I noticed an unfamiliar truck in the yard. I walked in, and there sat one of Dad's friends that I hadn't seen in two or three years. He congratulated me on the marriage and upcoming baby. Then, he asked how I was doing. We started talking about our cattle, and how to increase the milk production. When I left, he gave me a hug. The next morning, I finished cleaning up the barn and milking equipment, and went to the house. As I was making breakfast, I heard a truck pull in. I looked out and recognized Dad's friend with a stock trailer. As I ran out the door, he yelled, "Where do you want these unloaded?' I said, "You're not unloading anything. I haven't bought them, and I can't afford to buy groceries – much less cows!!!!" He looked at me and said, "My dear, if you recall – I didn't ask you about buying groceries. I asked you WHERE you want these cows unloaded. Now – I can open the doors here, but I would rather not see you have to chase them down in your present condition. But – if I have to I will. You can pay me a little whenever you can. I am not going to starve. And I am sure not going to stand by and watch this. I picked up these cows this morning and they are big, beautiful, and gentle. They are all in full lactation. So, now – where do I unload?" I almost said "Anywhere!!!", but I had him back up to the small door, and we led the four big, gorgeous, gentle creatures into the barn. I was crying and thanking him. No one had ever done anything like this for me – ever! He had searched for them, found them, picked them out, paid for them, and delivered them. Just for me. Unbelievable…

A few months later, Dad said he had some bad news for me. Unbeknownst to me, this man had been on kidney dialysis for a few years, and he had passed away during the night. I nearly collapsed to the floor. Oh NOOO!!! *Dear Lord!!!! You took my angel home. How am I ever going to pay him back now?* I flew into town to hunt up his business partner. I asked if I could pay him for the cows. He said "No – that was between him and you." I offered to pay the man's ex-wife. Again, I was told, "NO." Go home; enjoy the gifts he wanted you to have." I have not, nor will I ever forget him. Lord, I thank You for him and his concern for me. That was pure, unselfish love in motion. I have prayed that the sweet man knew the Lord.

A few months later, I had a discussion with a non-believing elderly gentleman about life after death. I asked him, "So – if there is no heaven or hell, what do you think happens after we die?" He said, "Well, I think we just end up wherever we were thinking about when we died." I had to process that for a minute and said "Well… I think you need to be praying that you don't die while you have the stomach flu …." That seemed a bit crazy to me. I explained to him that life has no complete end and began when God created it. And, he questioned my sanity. I said, "Think about this." A rock is dead. No matter how many rocks you put together, they will never reproduce. They are dead. Dead + dead = dead. You and I came from life. Before we were born, we were alive, or we couldn't grow.

*Dead things don't grow. The rocks don't grow. Pencils don't grow. We come 'to life' from life. Before conception, the "seeds" to create life are alive in our parents. And have been in every generation since Adam and Eve. We are conceived, grow, and are birthed from our mother's womb into this life. And at death, we are birthed into an eternal life. Life doesn't end. God gave us the ability to choose for ourselves where we will spend the next stage of life – a never–ending eternity, Heaven or hell. We have been given the options and the information to make the choice. God gave us the gift of free will. He wants us to choose Him, joyfully, thankfully. Philippians 2: 10-11 says "That at the name of Jesus every knee should bow…… And that every tongue should confess that Jesus Christ is Lord, to the glory of God the Father". That 'one day' will come. Whether you believe it or not. But there are so many blessings that are missed if we wait.*

As soon as I confessed it, and asked for His forgiveness of my sins, and please take control of my life, everything changed. I had peace, joy, and provision. I thank Him moment by moment for all His care.

One day a few years ago, one of my boys asked me "Why did God give people 'free will?'", as we were outside looking at the apple tree beginning to bloom. "It would be so much easier without it." He has three beautiful daughters, so I asked him, "Let's play out a little scenario…. Let's say that your youngest daughter came running to you with an apple from this tree in her precious little hand, shouting, 'DADDY, DADDY!!! Look what I just picked for you!' And with a big excited, joyful smile, bouncing up and down, waited to see if you liked it or not… Or…. She came dragging her feet with a dull, expressionless look and said, 'Here. I got an apple for you. Enjoy.' And turned around and walked away. Which one would you want?" He immediately said, "The first one!"

"Why?"

"Because I would know that she wanted to do it because she thought I would like it and didn't feel like she had to. It was because she loves me and wanted to give me something."

"BINGO." That's exactly why God gave us free will. So that we can choose Him joyfully, living in His promise and provision, knowing where we will spend stage 3 of our life, stage one is pre-birth, stage two is earthly life, and the third is eternal – never-ending – Hell, or Heaven with the One who created us and sent His only begotten Son to die to cover our sins. God chooses stage one and gives us life. We can't choose our genealogy, or how we are raised. We can choose what we do with our life, and how, and where we will live our adulthood. We also can choose where we will spend stage three. Stage one is approximately nine months, stage two can be any length, but the Bible says that the average is 70-80 years. Stage three is eternity. It will never end. I want to spend it forever in Heaven with Jesus and my Heavenly Father who has picked me up and made my life amazing and worthwhile.

Winter came with a roar. By Christmas, we had a lot of snow, and the temperatures were frigid. My husband's family always went out together on New Year's Eve. Since my baby wasn't due until the end of January, I went with them. By 11 p.m., I was not feeling well at all. I don't drink, and to me, bars were mostly loud and back then, smoke filled places filled with people doing things that they would probably regret later. This was no exception. I couldn't find my husband anywhere. Finally, a sister-in-law laughed. She said, "Go downstairs. There is a closet under the stairwell…" And she laughed again. I turned and carefully made my way down the steep, narrow flight of stairs. I saw a door, and cautiously reached for it. I felt sicker as I turned the knob. As I pulled it open, I saw him – with her in his arms - the woman that he had been in love with for years. I had known that there was 'someone', but now I had seen her with my own eyes. He asked me what I wanted. There were no words. I closed the door and slowly climbed the stairs. I asked a woman if she would take me home. She and her sister obliged. I don't know when he came home. My heart was broken, all hope was gone.

    The following Sunday night was frigidly cold. My husband wasn't feeling well, so I quietly went out and did the chores. I fed all the cattle silage and grain, cleaned and bedded their stalls, and managed to get the milking done before my water broke. I went back to the house, cleaned up, changed clothes, and called my parents to let them know. In case something happened to me, I just wanted someone to know. Mom said, "Hurry up and have it before midnight so it will be on my birthday." "MOM… It is after ten now. I don't have time!" My "other half" was still sound asleep. I went back through the frozen crunching snow to finish the chores, throw down hay and fill their mangers for the night, clean up the milking equipment, and milkhouse, etc. Later, my Godfather scolded me because I didn't call him. I didn't know that I could. I honestly thought that no one would care.

By five a.m., I had to get him up. I was in trouble. I needed to get to the hospital. One of his brothers came and did the chores that morning for us.

When we arrived at the hospital, we were met by my irate doctor. By noon, the contractions were back-to-back. There was no relief – no break. And, I still hadn't dilated much at all. I was given Pitocin, but it didn't help. At around two, my body pushed the baby through anyway. I heard voices screaming. I heard the doctor yelling at the nurses to do something! Then, he was screaming "I have lost her!!! We have lost her!!! She's gone." *Buddy – I am tougher than that….*

I have very few memories of the first three or four days after delivery. I know that my doctor canceled his clinic appointments and sat by my bed as much as he could. If he wasn't there, he made sure that an RN was. 24-7. I know this because they told me later how afraid he was for me. It turned out that apparently when I was in the car accident in Ohio, there were undetected internal injuries. He said that had he known, he would have done a c-section and a tubal. I said, "Its ok. I'll live. But – you, my dear – are extremely messy." He questioned that. I said, "When you were delivering my son, there was a huge trash can on each side of my feet. You couldn't hit either one with the towels or anything else. The room was a total mess. Walls and all! I feel bad for the poor people who had to clean that up! ".

"How do you know that????? You were unconscious."

I said, "I watched it all."

*"FROM WHERE????"*

I said, "I was up in the left-hand corner tight to the ceiling watching you! I was thinking, *Ohhhh wow! That looks horrible!!! I'm sure glad I am not her!!!!"* He went snow white. He said, "I knew it. I knew that I had lost you." "You can't get rid of me that easily my dear! I'm still here."

A friend later told me that in nursing school, the procedure that was used had been taught as 'last ditch' effort- right before they pronounced the patient dead. Oh, the great joys…. But it was worth it all! I had a beautiful baby boy! Thank You Lord for bringing us safely through this. Five days later, we were able to go home. *Now – maybe he would love me*, I had given him a son. For the first time in my life, I had hope that everything would be ok.

After healing, my doctor wanted to do a tubal ligation on me. I refused, because I wanted a baby girl. He said that –under no circumstances ever – would he deliver another baby for me. "I watched you nearly die once. I am not going through that again." (This doctor was the doctor who had delivered me and treated me as his own.) He insisted that since I couldn't take "the pill", he had to put in an IUD. I finally agreed. God forgive me – I had no clue how they worked. No one told me. As I understand – 'contraceptive' means 'to prevent' conception. Later, I found out that this thing allowed conception, but created an infection in the uterus so that the baby can't live. This still makes me sick if I stop to think about it. But – praises to my Lord – late that fall – I just knew that I was expecting another baby! So, I made an appointment with my doctor....

When he walked into the examination room, he asked, "What brings you in? Are you ok?" My husband had reluctantly come with me to hold our beautiful baby boy. I smiled and joyfully said, "I am pregnant." "NO, you are not." "Yes, I am." After a few slightly varied repetitions on the same theme, I said, "If you don't believe me – check me." So, he did. He stared at me in total disbelief. He got up and walked out of the room. A few minutes later, he was back. He said, "Be at the ER door ready at five am Thursday morning. I asked him "Why???" He said," A 'D&C', it is the only choice." I said, "OH NO. *There is NO way that I am killing my little girl."* (There were no ultrasound machines back then. But I knew she was a girl from the very beginning!) He proceeded to tell me that the IUD had grown into the side of my uterus. It was embedded there with my tiny helpless baby. The baby could not possibly survive with it there. It would end up tearing through the uterine wall and we could both die. So, I said, "Well, then take it out." Sounded simple.... He told me that if he did that, I would miscarry right there, on the table. I said, "Well, if that is God's will – so be it. I want to try." He said, "There is no way she could be normal with all that...." I said, "Define normal – no one will ever notice around here..." He had to laugh, admitted that I had a valid point, and agreed to try to remove it. Oh, Dear Lord. If I had thought giving birth was bad.... Someone later told me that he had been in town that day, and he didn't know what happened at the clinic, but they had heard a woman screaming clear on the other side of town!! I laid there, unable to move for over three hours before I could get up.

When I could finally get up, I was given very strict orders for complete bed rest. I was not to pick up or care for my son. No house cleaning or farm work. Go to bed. Go directly to bed and stay in bed. Until that baby is born. When I got home, I made arrangements with a neighbor's daughter to stay, care for the baby, cook, and clean.

I managed to stay in the bed for three whole days. I couldn't stand the sound of my crying baby, and the house was a total wreck. I asked God to protect us, and I got up. I stroked my baby girl in my tummy and told her, "Sweet baby girl – I love you! But I can't lay here for all these months. Life is hard, and you will have to be strong. So, sweet child – hang on! Here we go!" And go – we did! There was a severe drought that spring and summer. Our fields weren't growing much feed for the cattle. My husband got a job driving a bulk milk truck, so I did all the chores, and all the farm work. We needed the money to buy hay for the winter. I took baby boy with me, and he loved the cows!! They were so patient with him! Life and time flew by.

Around the expected due date, I was taking my little sister home after she had helped to watch the baby during chores for me when a deer came flying out of the woods. Even though I slammed on the brakes, I hit him. My little sister and the baby were shaken and scared, but ok. And – praises to God – the deer got up and ran away! I went into the clinic the next day for my scheduled appointment. (I had to see a different doctor since mine left town for a few weeks. He said he wasn't coming back until he got the call that my baby had been delivered. I laughed and told him not to forget that I was tough and that I would just hang on until he was home!!! "You can't stay gone forever…") The new doctor listened for her heartbeat. After several attempts, he looked up at me and said, "That baby is dead. We need to induce labor and get rid of it." "Oh…. Noooo…we are not doing anything like that at all. She is fine. She will come out on her own when she is good and ready. Until then – you are leaving her alone. Do you understand me???" Two weeks after that, I went into labor on a Wednesday morning. During those two weeks, I had never felt her move and no heartbeat had been detected. But I was praying. I waited until around eleven a.m. before I called the hospital. A woman I knew well answered. I asked her if my doctor was back. She said that it was a strange thing. The other doctor got sick the night before, so mine had to come back. He had just walked in!! Oh, my Lord has a great sense of humor and perfect timing!!! I said, "Well, don't tell him, but I am in labor and will be there in half an hour!" She laughed and promised not to. In a small town, everyone knows everything! I was able to sneak into the hospital and was in a bed before I heard him outside the door. He asked who the patient was. The nurse laughed and said, "Go see". He walked in and stared at me in disbelief. I smiled sweetly and said, "I told you I could wait." He was speechless. And honestly – we were both scared. But, at the end of the day, all was well. I had my baby girl! And, as proud as I was, I believe he was prouder – happier – and more relieved!!! She was, and is, strong, beautiful and healthy! Now, I was blessed with two amazing gifts from heaven!

Life is like a river, full of turns and changes. Life's circumstances took us off the big farm and onto a small 'hobby farm'. I planted a large garden, had a couple of cows for house milk, cats and a few dogs, a baby calf, and Miss Piggy. Back in the neighborhood where I grew up, I loved my life. I could take the kids and walk to my parent's farm to help them. It was almost a mile away, and I was thankful to be able to pull the kids in a little wagon and go help them. I have to admit that it was a little spooky walking back home in the dark through the heavily wooded lowlands. There were bears, coyotes, and who knows what else in there. But the kids and I would sing loudly, and God protected us. When I was given an amazing dog – another black Lab, he would pull the wagon with the kids in it. I never asked Dad for any payment at all. Ever. It was my joy to help them and be back on my home farm with the cows. I talked to my oldest child recently and he was talking about them bringing the calf and Miss Piggy into the house, eating supper, and having the calf or the horse come in to see what was going on. I laughed and said, "Yes, you guys left the door slightly open on purpose." God's critters are pretty smart and can figure things out if they want to badly enough.

He also reminded me of the time when Dad and Mom were out of town for a weekend getaway, and I was doing the chores for them. We had walked down and were trying to get done before it got really dark. But… My Dad had a love for ducks and geese. We all loved the chickens and ducks. But those wretched geese? Not so much. They stood almost as tall as my kids and were as mean as could be. They would "bite" or pinch and it was painful. They were tall enough that I was worried that they would peck the kids' faces or eyes. Plus, they would chase you and beat you with their wings. After rescuing the kids a few times, I said,

"Enough of this foolishness, I can't milk the cows and defend my kids at the same time. Something has to give."

So, I caught them, one by one and put rubber bands around their beaks and tied their feet loosely together so they could still swim and set them gently in the swimming pool. My plan was that as soon as I was done and had the kids safe and protected, that I would remove the geese from the pool and set them free.… But. I forgot. We got done. We went home. We went to bed. We went to sleep. Until around 2:30 in the morning. When the phone rang. My Daddy was beyond irate. I have never heard him like that. Ever. "Good grief Mya! Someone was here and vandalized the place!!!" "WHAT???" "You wouldn't believe what I found when I came home!!" By now, both kids were awake and had come running to hear what had happened to the farm. "I'm going to call the Sheriff's Department! This is horrible!" I got him calmed down a wee bit and asked what had happened, and what damage had been done. THEN he described the 'goose situation'.… Oops… "Well, Daddy, are they ok?" "YES, but who knows how long they had to sit in the water!" (I was thinking that God made them to do exactly that…) "Well Dad, I'm thinking that they'll be fine. And if everything else is ok, I'm thinking that the sheriff's department has far more pressing problems to deal with. He said that they were fine, and when he unrubberbanded them, they were just fine, and one actually jumped back into the pool.… When I hung up the phone, the kids and I were laughing so hard that we couldn't go back to sleep for hours! Many neighbors and friends, and my kids would have been much happier with a much different outcome.…

I was the organic and home-grown healthy food momma. Homemade bread, hand churned butter from our own fresh milk, and cinnamon rolls from scratch! My husband got a job in town. There were thunder clouds on the horizon, but I totally misread them then… I thought we were living the American dream… all the things that country music songs are written about.

A week before my daughters second birthday, a car pulled into the yard. Before I saw it, the kitchen door was opening. In walked 'my big teddy bear'. My legs wouldn't hold me. I had to sit down. He was holding a brand-new crying baby girl in his arms. He handed her to me. As I calmed her, he said, "This is my daughter. I am taking her home from the hospital. I stopped here because I wanted you to see her." I couldn't breathe – much less speak. I knew he had married, and we had all moved on. A few deep breaths later, I said, "Thank you for thinking of me. She is so beautiful!" He said, "My wife wants to go back to work as soon as possible. And, you are the only one who is going to take care of my child." *Ok – breathe. Take the high road. Show no fear. Show no pain. Walk on.* I heard myself say, "Sure, I would be happy to do that." Approximately two years later, she had a cute little baby brother. I treated them and loved them like my own. I could have no more children, so I thanked God for blessing me with these. His wife and I became very good friends. I have been greatly blessed by knowing her. Of all the women he could have married, I am glad he chose her. She stood by me many times when the rocks came up in my road.

Nine days before my daughter's third birthday, we were visiting a place where there were no indoor bathroom facilities available to me and my children. There was an old outhouse filled with mosquitoes. My little sister and I tried to make light of the situation and get my children in and out as quickly as possible. My poor little girl seemed to be covered with bites. She fared much worse than we did. A few days later, I made a doctor's appointment for her, and we went in. I was told that they were "just mosquito bites. Nothing to worry about." They weren't any better after another few days, so back I went only to hear the same story. After a couple more of these fruitless trips, I took her to the emergency room. By this time, she was admitted. She rapidly went downhill. The same doctor who had delivered her drew blood specimens. Since our small-town hospital had a very small lab, these were sent to a larger lab about 85 miles away. The results would not be back for days. Her tiny body was hugely swollen, and she would scream in pain if as much as a sheet touched her. Scarier yet was the moment when she no longer screamed. She was unrecognizable. I couldn't hold her or comfort her. I never left the room. A neighbor watched our son. And, since no one knew what was causing this – we were totally isolated from the world.

Then came the moment when the doctor said, "Call your pastor. She isn't going to make it. Her kidneys, liver, and heart are shutting down. We don't know what she has, so I can't treat it. By the time the results come back – she will be dead. But if I have your permission – I could try a very high dosage of a broad-spectrum antibiotic. It is the only thing that I can think of and the only chance that she has." I said, "Hurry up!!! Go get it!!! Start it now!!" And – he did. She was so far gone, that when he stuck the needle in to start the IV, she didn't move at all. Her eyelids didn't even show any movement. All I could do was pray and beg God to save my baby girl. And – praises to Him, He did!!! By the next day, when the lab called with the results – a bad staph infection...., she was opening her eyes!

We celebrated her third birthday in the hospital. A neighbor brought in a beautiful little cake with candles, the nurses sang to her, blew up the rubber gloves to look like 'chicken' balloons, and we all thanked God for saving her. An amazing neighbor lady went into our house and scrubbed and washed every square inch before I brought her home. I was so thankful!

The following year, we had new neighbors. She stopped by and said she heard that I took care of children, so I had hers also. At one point, the children in my care were aged 5, 4,3,2,1, and 6 months old. It was an amazing time for all of us. They followed me outside in the garden, helped hang clothes on the line, helped make and decorate cookies, etc. I remember one time when I was in the garden pulling weeds, and looked up to see the calf eating the corn plants, Miss Piggy rooting up the potatoes, the kids replanting the weeds 'so that they wouldn't die', and thinking *"So – why do I even try to plant a garden???"* And then my eyes filled with tears, and I said *"Father, forgive me, and Thank You Lord. This IS why I do it!"* We had a great time together. I was so blessed to hear their first words and to help them take their first steps.

I had bought my little ones a "kid's swimming pool", so, one hot summer day, I looked out the kitchen window and saw them brushing a very happy Miss Piggy with the toilet bowl brush as she laid sprawled out in the pool, and the dog was waiting his turn... It was hard to tell if the kids or Miss Piggy or the dogs enjoyed it the most!

Through those years, I remember lying in bed at night, quietly crying and asking God to fix our marriage. I prayed that if I could be a better wife, to show me what I was doing wrong. He didn't want to do anything with us. He was losing patience with me and our children. (The little ones were picked up before he came home, so most days, he didn't even see them.) I prayed that if I was doing something wrong to please fix me, show me. His temper would flare. Violent outbursts increased. He would tell me to put the kids to bed and get out of the house so that he didn't have to look at me. On weekends, he liked to go down to the local bar and sit and have a beer with the boys whenever he could.

On a Saturday evening when I was absolutely frazzled and couldn't see how I'd ever get through life, there was a knock on the door and an older cousin just walked in. He looked around at the situation and seen my husband laying on the sofa watching TV while I was trying to get the dishes done, floors swept, kids bathed, etc. He came a little bit unraveled and walked into the living room. He told my "other half" to get up and help me. "You have been on unemployment all winter, she's babysitting the neighbor kids, trying to help her parents, plus doing everything here. Get up right now. I'm taking her out, and when I get back, the house better be clean, dishes done, and the kids bathed and asleep." WOW. He looked back at me, and said, "Go clean up and change clothes." And "YES SIR!" I quickly did. He took me to a country music dance and treated me like a queen. He danced better than Rhett Butler in "Gone with the Wind"! He could have easily gone professional! At about 11:30, during a beautiful waltz, a couple of young men got into a fight up front, close to the band, so the band stopped playing. My cousin turned his head to see what happened. And said, "Excuse me for a minute." He went to them, grabbed each of them by the front of their shirts and lifted them up, with their feet clearing the floor. You should have seen the looks on their faces! He said, "Do I have your attention now??" Somehow, they squeaked out a feeble "yes". "OK. Do you see that beautiful woman there? Do you know what her life is like? I took her out for an enjoyable night and you two have ruined it for her. I am ashamed of you both. Now… If I let you down, are you going to act like gentleman and take this outside or do we have to finish it up right here?" They squeaked out that they would leave, so he set their feet back on the floor, and I don't think I have ever seen anyone run that fast! I don't think a scared rabbit could have kept up. It was an amazing night to remember. And, when we came home, the kids were asleep, the dishes were done, and all looked very good. It was the only time that he ever did it, but I was very thankful for that night, and my cousin.

He was a rather large, muscular man who had farmed and worked heavy equipment all his life. He had never married, and since he was five years younger than my Dad, they had grown up more as brothers than cousins. He had always been there for me all my life. When he was home, he would always stop to see me, and my kids loved him as much as I did. They would see his truck pull in and start jumping up and down! He tended to bring them things that I wouldn't want them to have. Like the day he showed up with three 5- gallon buckets of candy…. All I could do was tell him "NO", they don't need that. So, Smarty-pants that he was, he asked my kids. All six of them. Your Mom says that you don't need this. What's your opinion? Do you want to keep it?" Of course, they yelled "YES!!!" He looked at me and laughed his head off. Could barely stand up. He said, "They win. You're outnumbered."

This is the same man who, several years later had ordered a new Ford pickup and flew into Detroit to pick it up and drove it many miles- straight to me. I was working in a "three-piece suit", 3" heels, etc., very secure setting. One afternoon, I received a call from the main office. "Do you know a man by the name of…" "Yes, I do, why?" He's up here demanding to see you." "I'll be right up." I seen him, ran to him, and he gave me a big hug! Then he announced to the whole lobby, "I just bought a new F150, and I drove it down here because she's going to be the only other person who will ever drive it. She's leaving and won't be back until tomorrow. Deal with it." And turned to me and said, Go get your purse, because you need a good time." And a wonderful time it was! I still have a picture of him and that truck. He has always been a rock in the floods of my life. He was always there for me, and as his life is coming close to "stage 3" entrance, I pray that he has accepted Jesus as his Savior and has given his life to our Lord.

Everything came to a head when we were at "my big brother's" wedding. His bride had been asked me to straighten her train before she went down the aisle, and to help with a couple other things. I had assumed that since we were both invited, that we both would go, that's what married couples do. The evening of the wedding, I went and picked up the young lady who was going to babysit our children. When she and I got back, he said that he didn't want to go. I was surprised and asked why? He said to 'just take her' and he would stay home with the children. I was bewildered…. I asked him 'why' again. To this day, I wish I had done as he asked. He finally changed clothes and came with me. The wedding went well, the cake was cut, and on to the wedding dance. We both were talking with people that we hadn't seen in years, and I didn't notice when he disappeared. When the dance for the wedding party was announced, the groom said, "Go get your husband, we want you both here with us." He was in the bar, enjoying a drink with a beautiful young lady. I was told to leave. So, I did. Periodically, I would go check on him. I just wanted one dance, with my husband. I had already danced with Dad and some of my cousins. My heart was breaking. *Show no pain. Show no sorrow. Put your best foot forward. Turn up the music; rearrange the deck chairs....* the ship was going down. If asked, "Where is your husband?" I would say, "He is busy, he will be back in a few minutes......"

It was getting late; my parents had gone home, as had many others. I went back and asked him if I could please have the last dance with him. He told me "No. Can't you see that I am busy? Go sit in the car." So, I told a couple friends where I was going and said 'goodnight'. I got in the driver's side, locked the car doors, and must have fallen asleep.

I woke up at the sound of his pounding on the window. I quickly unlocked the door and tried to get up to go around to the passenger side. (He had been drinking..... Why did I automatically assume that he could still drive????) I was part way up when he hit me in the jaw. Immediately an upper cut hit the other side. I went back down into the car. Stunned, bewildered, and bleeding. I slid out the other side and ran into the building. I was met by my "big brother". He helped me get into the bathroom. I was crying hard. He asked what had happened. I told him. For the over eight weeks, I couldn't open my mouth. My jaws were permanently damaged.

The meal replacement type drinks couldn't be purchased in stores back then. They were only at the hospitals and nursing homes. And God through His infinite wisdom and mercy had the mother of two of the little ones in my care, working at a hospital. I don't know how I would have survived if not for her provision.

I never went to my doctor. I didn't want him to know what had happened. A police officer friend wanted me to press charges. I said – no. If I did, there would be no hope of fixing the marriage. He said he was sorry that this had happened, but it did nothing to bring us closer. I realized that there are two kinds of lonely. One kind finds me sitting on the sofa all alone and lonely. The other kind has someone sitting beside me on the sofa, and I am still totally alone. I felt abandoned, lost and rejected. I so badly just wanted someone to love me. I wanted to feel accepted for who I was. I wanted the hurt to go away. I had the children, and I was very grateful for them, but I was empty and hurting.

My Dad told me that if I lost weight, dressed better, cooked better, kept the kids quieter, kept house better, etc., he would quit hurting me…. I tried all of that. How could I know where the bar was on that? How good did I have to be? How much of all that was enough? I never did get it right apparently. I thank God that His love for us isn't based on good deeds well done. We would never know if we were good enough. No one would ever make it into heaven. If a few did manage to slide in as the gate slammed shut, their tail feathers would be smoking.

I tried everything I could think of to interest him in me. Everything I did – failed. He would laugh at me and ask, "Who do you think that you are? Miss America? Don't waste money on clothes. You can't change the fact that you are fat and ugly by putting on different clothes and buying makeup." Nothing I did made any difference. Nothing helped at all.

When the kids and I went to church, I would see families sitting together. The husband would have his arm, lovingly and protectively around his wife, while she would turn her peaceful, contented face up to meet his eyes and smile. And their kids would sit there all full of smiles. And there, I sat – alone. It hurt. *Lord – why – what am I doing wrong*? He didn't answer me.

As I read about Jacob and Leah in Genesis, I can identify with her pain. But she was the mother of Levi and Judah. Jesus is "the Lion of the tribe of Judah." God blessed her greatly. Out of my pain and rejection, I made mistakes. I just wanted someone to love me, I had never had a "safe place". Again – people see what you do – God knows why you did it.

Life was moving my first baby girl on. She graduated from high school on a Friday night, got married Saturday night, and on Sunday morning, moved to the west coast. My world just became a whole lot emptier. This emptiness brought my mother and me closer. I was very thankful for that.

When my daughter went into first grade, I got a job in town. We simply needed more income. Then, we made one of those life changing decisions. We sold our little peaceful farm on a land contract and moved into town, so I could walk to work. Dad's idea… not ours. He said that we would save more money on gas and car expenses. He still held sway over a large part of my life. I tried to get through to him that our farm was paid for. We had no mortgage. And the "money that we saved on gas" would never cover a mortgage payment. If we moved into town, we would be in debt again. To no avail. He had never had debt of any kind, so he didn't realize the load it creates. He had saved up cash, and paid Grampa for the farm.

The kids and I hated living in town. We were country – born and bred – as they say. They had to change schools. It was not good for any of us. I was still helping on the farm and had to drive back and forth for that. There was just too much work for my parents.

I wish I had learned earlier that when one is conned or manipulated to achieve the manipulator's plans and goals, the manipulated are being deemed unfit to choose their own life and make their own decisions.

One summer morning, Dad had called and asked if we could come out and help him with the haying. Since I had a few more hours before I got off work, my husband took our children and went out. Later, a friend and I followed. We were slowing to a stop to turn left onto a county road with a couple cars behind us, when an out of state car flew around all of us and hit the driver's front side at a very high rate of speed. It spun my 77 Ford Thunder Bird (another heavy lead sled with a full solid steel frame) around and sent the other car off the road. (Dad had been criticizing my choice of vehicles as needing to be "more logical, economical, practical, etc.…) I called the police, and my parents. They all came. Had my car been smaller, it may well have been deadly. I asked dad what he thought about it now… He said, "I'm wondering where we can get you a Sherman tank." I thank God that He sent my kids and their dad out first to protect them. I love seeing how He works things out for good.

I was diagnosed with torn disks, torn rotator cuffs, etc. I kept working. *Why stop now. Keep walking. Keep going. Show no pain.* As the pain became worse, facet joint nerve blocks were done. Ohhh…… really great joys. I had to travel to a huge hospital about three hours away. My husband wouldn't go with me, so Mom and an uncle went since I couldn't drive after the long miserable procedure. This was so much worse than childbearing pain. But, when it was over, the unpleasant doctor said that I was the only one who had ever made it all the way through the complete procedure. No one had been able to take the pain. I guess God used the pain in my past to get me through this. I was supposed to stay home on bed rest for a few days, but I would have lost my job. So, the next morning I got up, slowly walked to work, crawled down the stairs to my office and carried on as best I could.

Nothing was helping, the pain and pressure increased, and the marriage disintegrated. The kids and I found an unfinished house in the country. My best friend and I finished it, and the kids and I moved in. In the divorce, I asked for "the kids, the cat, my car, the guinea pig, our clothes, and my cassette tapes that I had before we got married." I left him with the furniture, the house and the hobby farm that I had had to pay the attorney's fees on to repossess. The land contract holders had walked out on it. I took nothing from him. What good is 'stuff' if there is no love with it? I didn't want to bring left over hurt into what I hoped would be a clean start.

My mother and I had a much closer relationship after the grand children were born. I was very grateful to God for that. I never realized that we were 'all she had'. She went to an auction and bought on older- but like new sectional sofa for me for $75.00. She was so proud when she came by and told me. We had no furniture at that point. That was the first furniture for our new house.

The kids still tease me about turning on the light and hearing the toilet flush! I had tried my hand at wiring…. I thought I had done a great job until they turned on the three-way switch by the front door and the vent fan in the bathroom came on….so I hired an electrician…. A friend volunteered to help me hang the kitchen cabinets for payment of a bucket of chicken from a local restaurant. We learned about plumbing, PVC pipe, and the purple stinky stuff that goes with it. We worked hard, and thanked God for the house and a new start.

Late that fall, I was serving at a community barbecue when a man I knew from work asked what I was doing that night. I said I was going out with mom and dad. I figured that I was safe. I had long since adopted a system of giving 'forward' males the number to the local police department or a local bank if they wouldn't go away. This was a respectable man who had his own business and had recently broken off an engagement. So, he said that he might meet us there. We had a great time, and he took me home - at Dad's suggestion.... He went to church, was good to my children, and to me. I was joyful. My best friend went to work for him, all seemed to be well. He proposed, I accepted, and he gave me a very pretty ring. Since I hadn't had a ring the first time, I was impressed with his sincerity. We set a date for late in the year, because, I had a major back surgery scheduled for the first part of the next year. I kept asking him, "What If I can't walk afterwards??? What if I can't work? What if all we have is your income? What if they are right that I may not ever be able to do anything again?" I covered all the 'what ifs' that I could think of.... Many times.... He repeatedly answered them all reassuringly.

One Saturday, shortly before the wedding, he called and asked me if I would bring him lunch. I said, "Of course!" As I was working in the kitchen, I saw a pile of papers on the counter. I glanced at them. *Ohhh noooooo... they were all bills.... All overdue.... Huge amounts.... That explained a lot....* I was crushed. I asked him why he hadn't told me. He said that it was none of my business. But it was. My children's lives were at stake.

I drove, crying, out to my parent's farm. I tearfully told them what I had found. I said that I couldn't afford to pay the bills and that his vehicles were in repo. I had to cancel the wedding. My dad said, "If that wedding is canceled, it is because he has opened his eyes. I can see why someone would want to shack up with you - but marry something like you – never. If you cancel it, we are done with you." So, I sucked it up and went on. I co-signed for loans, used my home as collateral, and went on. I set up payment schedules with his creditors, put my shoulder to the wheel and pressed on.

The wedding came and went. My surgery date arrived. I checked into the hospital very early. Went to the operating room about 5 a.m. and didn't come out until around 8:30 p.m. They told me that my blood pressure kept dropping so low that they finally had to quit. There were solid fusions and laminectomies from my waist to my tailbone, and Steffi plates installed with screws that looked just like the ones in our barn doors. I didn't know that there was a "bone bank" like there is a blood bank. I was told that some of that was used, and they 'harvested' ¾ of a cup of bone from my hip.... And there was a lot of pain. I couldn't move for a few days. This was ok with me.... If I moved it hurt... If I breathed, it hurt.... By the time I could sit up, I would get dizzy and pass out. *Gracious Lord – I will get through this somehow....* My poor children. They went from having a fully functioning mother who could go sliding with them to this....

I was told that I'd never walk again. But I was determined that I would. A seemingly long time passed before I could go home. I struggled. I couldn't roll over in bed by myself, couldn't walk without a walker. I couldn't pick it up to take a step – I had to 'crab-crawl' it – no wheels back then... My friend who was a nurse, got me into the shower, took off the rigid back brace, bathed, dried, and replaced it before I could get out of the tub. I will never forget her selfless love and concern for me, and I thank God for her! And, I wasn't supposed to drive for six months, and then only after a re-evaluation.

Between Mom and my friends, the housework was done, and I was beginning to get up by myself with the help of the walker and started being an asset – not a total liability to my family. The kids laughed so hard when I learned how to pick things up off the floor with my toes. They would roll a pencil off the table occasionally just to watch me pick it up and place it back on the table. There was a lot less pain involved, and I couldn't bend over anyway. Things weren't healing well, so I was fitted for a body cast. It was a hard, thick white plastic solid form from the base of my neck to my tailbone in the back, coming together tightly in the front. It was so very uncomfortable, hot, itchy, and all around – a total delight...

Somewhere during this recovery time, I received a phone call from a jewelry store asking if this number was a contact for my husband. I said, "Yes, why?" Well, it turned out that the ring I had been given to show his love for me had been given to someone else a few years earlier, and still hadn't been paid for. Did I want them to repo it or did I want to pay for it? As I swallowed the tears, I agreed to pay for it. So, I did have a ring this time, but I had to pay for it. Dad's words, "Blessed are those who have low expectations, for they shall not be disappointed" rang in my ears.... It would be ok. I loved him, and no one is perfect. Life happens. I remember wishing that he had been honest and told me.

There was no way I could hold out for the whole six – no driving allowed-month thing. The kids helped me get out and into the car and we went for lunch! I never realized how heavy public entrance doors were until then. There were very few automatic doors then. They had to open the doors, help me sit down, get up, go to the bathroom, etc. Thank You Heavenly Father for my children!

When my older sister and I were little, our Grandmother would order her garden seeds from a catalog. And, for one penny, she ordered a 'kid's seed packet'. It was a delightful mix of seeds of all sorts. (I always thought that they swept the floor at the end of the day and divided the sweepings into the packets!!) Some seeds were recognizable, some were total surprises. Grandma would explain that since we didn't know what they were, they needed to be planted in the sunshine, watered, weeded, and given the best possible care. As they grew, we would eventually see what God intended them to be. Then, if they needed shade – transplant them. If they were climbers – stake them up.

I believe the same basic principle works with children. When we hold newborns in our arms, we have no idea who or what they will be when they are grown. I always told my kids this story. When one grandchild was a newborn, his daddy called me and said that they couldn't get him to stop crying. I asked him, "What are you doing to that poor child?" He said, "Grandma – I think we are growing weeds!!!!" He had listened to me years before! I laughed, and all was well! God doesn't make 'bad' kids.... We do. So sad.

Within a year, my husband's business had new ownership, and we sold the house, used almost all the proceeds to pay off his debts, and moved far away. I never realized how devastating this move would be for my mother. We were all that she had. My back had not healed as well as expected, and I was unable to go back to work. My husband's job was winding down in a small town with few other opportunities. He had a family member who offered him a job, so we left. It seemed logical, but had my mother asked us to stay – I would not have left. God forgive me. I never thought about how our moving would impact her life.

A clean new start in life seemed like a great thing. We loved our new home! So beautiful, so friendly, and our neighbors were great. With a lot of kids at the house, I was very happy. My husband seemed to like his job, and we were off to a great start. Have you ever noticed that when you are happy, you tend to give an 'okay' to more things than you should because you want your partner happy also? I have always tried to be fiscally conservative and try not to spend beyond my means. But, being the compliant type of wife, I quietly watched him spend the money I had saved on things that were way out of my comfort zone. His family had told me that he had "champagne tastes on a beer budget". I just wanted him happy. And I knew that I wasn't making him happy. I knew that I couldn't grow hair, but I had received my medical records. At my heaviest point, right before I gave birth to my daughter, I had weighed 247#. It said, "patient has obesity." I thought "Oh no. Not for long." I was determined to change that. I went on what my kids called the "If it tastes good – spit it out diet". I lost 95# from that high point. I was ecstatic! For the first time in my life, I wasn't totally ashamed of myself. I thought that he would find me more attractive…. Only after I had reached my goal, did he tell me that he liked 'heavy set' women who dressed expensively. I couldn't win for losing. Literally. Add to that – I've always been a "forever in blue jeans" kind of girl (who really likes flip-flops….).

A series of misunderstandings and changes undermined the foundation of our marriage. And a second major back surgery didn't help. His new job began to keep him out of town, and he entered into a lifestyle that didn't include us. After four years or so, his company relocated out of state. We had to leave a place that I had grown to love dearly. This is where I discovered – to my children's dismay – that God had given me the ability to cry nonstop for over seven hundred miles.

Upon arrival in a completely different culture – that we came to appreciate with time – we struggled to adjust from living in a beautiful condo surrounded by palm trees to living in a travel trailer and walking to the campground's bathroom for showers, bathroom, etc. My son was old enough now to have a part time job, so, that left my daughter and me to try to figure it all out. We found a house to rent, but upon arrival, it was uninhabitable. Plan B. I went back to college, and we found a house in a smaller town closer to the college. My husband stayed where he was since he was only home a couple days a week. His interests were changing, and they didn't include us. So, I became engrossed in college, trying to cover another failure in my life. Nothing I said or did seemed to help.

The marriage collapsed. Again, I felt like a failure and made more mistakes. I was not a good example to my children. I prayed, but I didn't know that I needed to ask Him to forgive me, lead me, and guide me according to His will, His purposes and His plans. I just kept asking Him to change me because I knew that I was 'no good'.

But – Praises to my Lord – those years were such a huge blessing to me. Our new neighborhood was full of kids who ended up at our house. Some stayed a night now and then, some stayed for a few years. They knew that they were loved, wanted, and would be treated exactly like my own. Some nights there would be 20-27 kids there, mostly boys. Sadly, some precious children are born to parents who lose interest in parenthood or become unable to provide materially or mentally for them. Then the children end up on the streets, on their own – thinking that they are worthless and that no one cares. They didn't have that problem at my house…

The first one came a few nights before Christmas. My two had gone back south to see their friends over the holidays. I stayed because I had homework!!! At my age???

When I had told my dad that I was going back to college, he said," Do you have any idea how old you will be when you graduate????" I said, "So Dad – how old will I be in four years if I don't graduate???" He said that if I felt like I had to make a fool of myself - go ahead. I was over 21 and he couldn't stop me. But he reminded me that I wasn't too bright and probably wouldn't do well. When all was said and done, I had made the Dean's list and graduated with honors!!!

One late night I was sitting at my desk typing a paper. I was thanking God for the peace I now had, and occasionally watched the snowflakes gently falling. I heard something at the patio door. I looked up to see a young man slowly slide to the ground. I ran, opened the door and helped him up. He looked at me and asked if this was where my daughter lived. I said, "Yes, are you ok, can you walk?" He said that she had told him that I loved kids. Truer words were never spoken.

I turned on the oven, moved a kitchen chair to it, and put his feet on the oven door to warm them up. He had walked barefoot in pajamas over a mile to get to our house. I ran upstairs to get some of my son's clothes for him and while he went to change, I heated some soup. We talked for hours. He stayed most of the time for the next several years.

I look back at how God provided for all of us in awestruck wonder. I remember driving home one night and praying. I said, "Lord, when I get home, there will be a houseful of hungry kids. Father, You know that last night we cleaned out under the sofa cushions, under the beds and car seats. I have nothing left to feed them. Father, if You want these precious kids to eat, You have to provide. Lord, we are in Your hands."

I pulled into the driveway and stopped at the mailbox. There was a check for $89.00 from my mortgage company. They had issued a refund on escrow. In the fall. Before taxes and insurance were paid. I wasn't asking any questions! I was thanking my God and honking the horn!!! My beautiful daughter ran out of the house in a panic! I said, "Grab a couple of the boys!!! God provided!!! We have money!!!" They came running out, jumped into the car, and off we went to Sam's Club to buy macaroni and cheese, green beans, hot dogs, large boxes of cereal and lots of milk. At fifteen, that girl had the ability to organize and dispatch a formidable army.

We were very grateful that all the kids were fed. These years were and still are very precious to me. I wasn't living the way that I should have been, but – again – people see what you do. God knows why you did it. I made precious memories with these kids that I cherish to this day. I am still in contact with many of them. And I love their children!

These amazing years were filled with a lot of studying. I was in my late 30's and returning to college. I hadn't been allowed to take biology, chemistry, typing, or bookkeeping in high school because Dad thought that I would never need it and was too 'stupid'. But – one can't get a Bachelor of Science without taking science. And that was where my kids all stepped in. My son was my tutor for all things algebraic and scientific and my daughter could type as fast as I could talk. Praise You my Lord for those blessings!!!!! Many nights they worked with me late into the night.

Besides helping me, my daughter organized a tutoring system for the twenty some boys at the house connecting those strong in an area to those who weren't. And every report card was checked and accounted for. If they were in my house – they were expected to study and have good grades. They would say "My mom never checked my report cards." I would say," Well, you're here. And – I care! I want you to do well. Hand them over!" One thing I wish I had done differently is the major that I chose. The boys begged me to be a high school guidance counselor. I should have listened.

After a couple years of being single and the kids taking Mom to the movies with them because they didn't want me working all the time, they started telling me that I shouldn't be 'alone'. Alone??? In this house filled with all these kids???

I remember an attorney friend walking in one time staring in amazement. "Whose are all these kids???" They all said "Hers!" as they pointed at me. Then he watched in amazement as my daughter was pouring the last of many boxes of macaroni and cheese into a canning kettle, a couple boys putting hotdogs on the grill, and another one was opening cans of vegetables. He was amazed at how well they all worked together and there was no fighting. They all had jobs, the house was always clean with laundry done and folded.

They were all loved and valued. And – they knew it. He asked me if I had a dollar. I looked at him, laughed, and said "NO, I feed kids." One of the boys had one and gave it to him. He wrote on a piece of paper that he was on retainer if I ever needed him for anything. But I never did. My kids were amazing!

One evening, one of them brought home a man that they knew. Through him, I found out about two more boys whose mother had died when they were very young. There were no family members who would take them. They were the children of one of his cousins. They were about to be separated and sent to boys' homes. They were all each other had. I told my two about them. I asked, "What do we do?" They asked if I had seen them. No. Do they drink? Don't know. Do they smoke? No idea. What do you know? I do know that they need a home. Well then, bring them home. What are two more boys? Thank You Heavenly Father! I love my kids!!!!

We didn't meet them until the night they were brought to their new home. They didn't know us. They were terrified. I will never forget their faces. The older one stood slightly- protectively - in front of his little brother. I could see their fear and uncertainty. I could see that they had been through things that children should never have to go through. We tried to ease their fears.

My ever so practical daughter went through their little plastic grocery sacks of clothes. She turned to me and said "Mom. They need new clothes." I'm thinking *with what????* But – into the car and off to the store we went.

Again – thank You Lord! You made a way where there seemed to be no way. And my two youngest headed to school with brand new clothes. They adjusted quite easily to living with me and all the other kids. They were a great joy and blessing to me, and still are. But their cousin who I was seeing had custody of them.

He wanted to marry me. I said "No." There were serious issues. Then came a court date to see if all was going well. The Judge asked him how he was handling them. He said that they were living with me.

The Judge stated that since he had custody, if they were to continue living with me, he had to live there also and be married. He asked if I was in the courtroom. I was asked to come forward. And it was explained all over again. My heart sunk. My head was in a noose, and they were kicking the chair. We were given a short time to work out the details. He threatened to take the boys from me if I didn't marry him. He would get drunk and crazy and threaten to harm them and me. When he was sober, he was a wonderful man. Add alcohol – an instant transformation to terrifying. I was afraid of both scenarios. What would happen to my helpless and defenseless boys alone with his alcoholism and what would happen to me if I married him? The morning of the 'wedding day', he screamed and yelled at me because he had done something terribly wrong and yelling at me seemed to clear his conscience somehow. (Back to my intuitive five-year-old son asking why the one who is the 'wrongest' yells the loudest….) He told me if I didn't marry him, I would never see the boys again. He was using them to emotionally blackmail me. I said "If you think I'm going to marry you – you are completely out of your mind! Get out of this house!"

He left, and I turned around. Hiding inside the door of the next room were the most frightened and terrified boys I have ever seen. They cautiously stepped into the hallway. The older brother was again shielding the terrified younger one. He looked at me and said "What about us Momma?? What is going to happen to us???" My heart broke. Jesus died for me. I had to protect these precious boys who had already endured so much. Heart in my throat – trying to make the best of it – I said, "I do." This was the beginning of what a friend described as "a hayride through hell…".

Anyone who has experienced domestic violence know the abuse cycles. From the "I am so sorry" to short term peace and back around. A continual rollercoaster ride. Ups and downs punctuated by unfaithfulness and outbursts followed by forgiveness. One that stands out was when one of my boys came home from work quite late and knocked on my bedroom door to see if I was still awake.

He came in, sat on the edge of the bed and told me that the truck was parked outside the local pay by the hour – 'no tell motel'. I said, "Thanks", and got up. He said "Oh no Mom. You're not going alone." I assured him that I would be fine, and I left. I drove in and, sure enough, there was his truck. So, I wrote a note saying "Sweetheart, if you want breakfast in the morning, you'll need to stop and get bread, milk and orange juice. We are out, and you have the checkbook. I love you!" (And, I did. To this day, he is always in my prayers.) I signed my name and tucked it under the windshield wiper.

And – he came home at 4:30 a.m. Over being drunk. Smelling like cheap perfume. Red lipstick everywhere. And mad as a hornet at me. I was stalking him. I was 'interfering in his business'. He just had to be with a woman with long flowing hair that smelled like fresh shampoo. And I got beaten. I still loved him, but I sure didn't like him much at that moment… It never ceases to amaze me how alcohol can completely transform people. Sober, he would hold me and tell me that I was all that stood between him and Satan. He said that if I ever left him, that the devil would 'take him down'. We went to marriage counseling, but to no avail.

During all the drama, my children had graduated from high school, and I graduated with my Bachelor's degree. One went on to college, and one into military service. We moved to a neighboring state, so I could enter graduate school. I was doing well when I was in another auto accident. I had a beautiful 1986 Olds Cutlass. I had found it on my birthday sitting on the back row of a car lot. I remember squealing to a stop and doing a U-turn in the road. The man said that an elderly couple had bought it new, and the husband had recently passed away. She asked him if he would sell it for her. It felt and still smelled like brand new. It was gorgeous and ran beautifully! I grabbed it!

One night I had an eerie feeling. I called my daughter and told her I thought that I was going to be in another car accident. We talked for a while. She said to call her when it was over and to let her know that I was ok.

On the evening that I was heading in to take my mid-terms, a 1980's Mercury Grand Marquis - huge heavy lead sled – ran a red light, hit me hard, and I did a 360 and stopped at a still green arrow. The woman got out and started yelling at ME. With a multitude of witnesses, she quickly backed off. I couldn't get out of the car. My beautiful Olds was totaled. My injuries resulted in Fentanyl injections in my spinal cord for pain, and about a year later, a third back surgery.

All these events put increased stress on an already stressed marriage. One night, the phone was pulled from the wall in an angry rage. He told me that I had 30 seconds to dial 911 before he killed me. He had me –back to the wall-with his hand at my throat. I calmly said "I couldn't if I wanted to. The phone is already on the floor. So, go ahead. It's a win-win for me. I go home to Jesus, and you go to jail. Do what you need to do."

He threw me to the floor and left for a few days. I had lived for years with 911 pre-dialed, so all I had to do was pick up the receiver and hit "redial", and a spare set of keys under the seat of my unlocked car for a hasty escape if needed. There were times when I didn't want to go on. I couldn't see a way out. One really bad Friday afternoon, when we went to the bank so he could cash his paycheck, and they wouldn't cash it, violence broke out in the car on the way home. It wasn't my fault, I didn't write the check, and I'm not the bank. I had no way out of this, and there was an oncoming semi flying towards my car. Having no hope of ever getting out of this horrible situation, seeing no use for me in this world at all, of no value to anyone, I jerked the steering wheel in the semi's direction. Instantly – I seen a flash of a man's face. A former pastor, neighbor, and friend from many years ago. And – again – instantly, the semi driver and I turned our steering wheels away. We missed each other by mere inches. I thanked God for sparing our lives, and forgiveness for probably scaring the semi driver.

God had given me an amazing gift to accompany me through these tumultuous days. I had a beautiful cat who was extraordinarily smart. She could turn the TV on with the remote and flip channels until she came to her favorite wildlife channel. Then she'd lay on the coffee table and watch the action with her tail twitching back and forth. My husband loved her and would never have hurt her. She was my "watch woman". If she was sitting on the back of the sofa in the living room window with a stressed look on her face, I knew we were in for a rough time. If she was laying comfortably, sprawled out, or not visible, all was well. When he did get violent, she would try to get between us, and distract him. She was much braver than I was.

After too many slightly varied repeats of the same performance, God used an amazing, brave young man from the local sheriff's department to cuff him and stuff him into the squad car in a way that made television heroes look weak and ineffective. God used this young officer to save my life. To this day, I thank You my Lord for Robert. We are still in contact, an amazing man, his beautiful wife and wonderful kids. He is constantly in my prayers.

That state treated domestic violence in a very serious manner. The offender had to leave the state, and if the marriage was to resume after a year, the couple had to go to counseling. We tried to repair it, but the divorce went through anyway. A friend had begged me to leave him years before. But I didn't want another failed marriage on my record. I told him that I had said "Til death do we part." He had said "That well may happen." But – thanks to God and Robert – I lived on.

There will be peace in the valley one day, but it didn't happen then. My doctor found that bone fragments were interfering with my spinal cord, and he needed to correct it fast. I only needed to finish two classes at that time, and I would have had my Master's degree. But it wasn't to happen. After my third back surgery, and time out, I couldn't afford to finish.

I remember calling Dad and asking him if I could come home. I was basically homeless. He said no because I was a failure and an embarrassment to them. What would the neighbors think? Oddly, he had always seen that as the controlling interest in his activities. I moved in with a neighbor for a year while recovering from surgery and tried to regroup and find my way.

God, in His mercy and grace, provided a job for me and I started a new life. More blessings, another mistake. When I was hired, they did an extensive background check. The sweetest lady talked to me about it.

She asked me about the marriages. She asked me if I knew that I was the common denominator. She was trying to get me to see that I was the problem and assumed that I hadn't figured it out yet. I told her that I knew I was. I told her that they all said that they 'loved' me and couldn't live without me. They knew about the hair issue up front. Some things one can't hide, and I never tried. They promised that it wouldn't matter at all. It wasn't who I was. It was a 'condition' that I had. But, after a period of time which ranged from a few days to a year, it did matter. I heard "It didn't mean anything to me. It was just sex". Well – guess what honey? It sure meant something to me. If it happened once, it always was easier the next time. There was always hurt, discord, and distrust. These eat away at the very heart of a marriage. I looked at her and said "Well, at least, you can see that I keep trying... I don't quit. I don't give up."

I loved my job and was blessed with many great co-workers. One amazing older lady discovered that I shared her love of southern gospel music and would bring me cassette tapes which played continually in my office. People would come in, sit down, eat a handful of animal crackers from the jar on my desk, get up and leave. They didn't need anything but a moment of peace which I was happy to provide. I still had hope that someone would love me for who I was. Not for what I looked like. I never realized that Jesus already did.

All these years I had been praying for Him to fix me. I knew that I was the problem. I really didn't need people to keep pointing this out for me. I guess they thought they were trying to help. I never told anyone all the details. That would have hurt too deeply. I didn't want to be pitied. I just wanted to be loved. I kept praying that Dad's assessment of me had been wrong.

Many years later, I reread John 4:7-42. Jesus met a Samaritan woman and HE spoke to her first. HE initiated the conversation. HE asked her for a drink of water as a way of opening the door for an eternal life conversation. HE made a statement about her that He already knew the answer to. This let her know that HE already knew her and her past. HE didn't condemn her. HE spoke to her as if she was just as valuable to Him as anyone else. Thank You Jesus!!!! In verse 23, He states that the Father is looking for those who will worship Him in spirit and in truth. Again, people see what you do, but God sees your heart.

My time at this treasured job brought one more short marriage that was annulled when I was thrown out because I began to have severe numbness in my legs from pressure on the spinal cord again. I went to a University hospital where the chief orthopedic doctor stated that nothing could be done and that I needed to quit working immediately. My beloved said that he didn't care if I ended up in a wheelchair permanently. The doctor looked at me and said "Sweetheart – you need a new husband." I thought "If you only knew…." I was given thirty days to "wrap it up" and resign.

So, I followed my doctor's orders. And… he quit his job. If I "could sit home all day and do nothing" – so could he. The alcohol intake and verbal abuse grew. Again- God intervened about the time I had lost all my strength, my will, and this time, my desire to live. If he threw me out – I would truly be homeless.

One really horrible night when I just wanted it all to be over, God prompted a woman I had known from way back in that little country church to call me. She said that I had been on her mind and knew that she had to find me. She had a hard time getting my number. There were not many cell phones then and I had moved again. I heard her voice and started to cry. We hadn't talked for quite a few years. God used her as a knot in the end of my rope……. Someone to hold onto….

She asked if I could drive home. I could live with her. I told her that I couldn't leave yet, there were 'loose ends' to tie up. God moved again.

There was a death in the family, and I had to fly home. I was there for a week and flew back. It was worse. He wasn't going to have a woman that he had to support. God intervened again.

Mom called. She needed help for a couple weeks. She said that if I could fly back home, she would buy my ticket. He thought that was a great idea, so I went. I was there for two weeks. I stayed with my parents and my friend and her family.

When I flew back, I was met at the airport only to find that I had been thrown out of the house. All my belongings were in my car at the airport. It was over in less than a year, so even though he had filed divorce papers, the judge ruled it an annulment.

I never chose a husband. They chose me. I always thought that I could make it work this time if I just tried harder. *This one will love me. This one will stay and hold me. This time I will be ok.*

All I ever wanted was a husband who loved me, and loved me enough to not spend his time comparing me and my faults to all the beautiful women in this world. I couldn't compete if I had wanted to – which I definitely had no desire to do. If something isn't freely given,

I don't see much point in having it. And, now I know that for me, and perhaps others also, I would never settle for someone who "I think I can live with", I would have waited for the one "I can't live without". When I read how God created man and woman, He made Adam first, realized the guy was lonely and empty, He took a piece of Adam's rib and made one woman. If I had realized the depth of that earlier, I would never let Dad push me into anything. I'd have waited until I found the ONE God had made for me, or made me for. My "other half." But, then I wouldn't have my children, so God still worked it all out for good.

*Dads! – Treat your daughters like you want their husbands to treat them. Set the bar high. And hold it there. And hold them. Let them know that they are your very precious daughters, and the daughters of the most high God. Protect them so that they know their own worth. Raise your sons to be the best husbands and fathers that their families can rely on. Be the best example of who you want your child to be. It is a heavy, but so very blessed calling to be a husband and Father to a new generation.*

*My Mother or Dad never held me, hugged me, or said "I love you." It simply didn't ever happen. My older sister was blessed to have her grandparents who freely expressed their love for her. And I showered my little sister and my children with love from conception or the first moment I saw them – depending on how God delivered them to me!*

*Parents, your words to your children will echo through their minds for the rest of their lives. Make them sweet and positive. But – teach them right from wrong. It will give them strong core values on which to make good choices. It is easier to do it right in the beginning than to try fixing broken, hurting, wounded adults. A strong, sturdy house is hard to build on a shaky foundation.*

*I have always loved to go for walks. And as I've walked the streets in the neighborhoods where I have lived, I have wondered how many houses have happy families inside. And, if the houses were made of glass – transparent – would the behaviors of the inhabitants change? Are there things inside these walls and doors that would change if Jesus knocked on the door? Would we throw what we were reading or playing under the sofa? Would we turn the channel? If He walked in, what would He see that would bring Him glory and honor – or break His heart? But wait. He is already there. He already knows. He already sees. We can't hide anything from Him. As I walk, I try to pray for each person individually and the family as a whole in each home.*

Once again, I was broke, broken, but, ever hopeful. More drama and failure. But – I could feel a stronger pull on my heart towards God, but I still didn't know how to get to where I wanted to be. Another marital mistake. I asked him once "Why didn't you tell me that this is how it would be if I married you?" He laughed his loudest and said "You are so stupid. If I had, you would have never married me!" He was definitely right about that.

During this time, I asked someone who was very hard on me why they treated me like that. I was told, "Because you never retaliate. You never pay back. You love unconditionally. We can treat you badly and know that you will still love us." I said "Yes, I will. But please stop." Looking back – I did see warning flags up and waving, but I thought that with enough love, it would be ok. I was praying, going to a small country church, and knew that things were so wrong.

One Sunday morning, in the fall of 2006, our pastor was out of town. I went alone and felt completely alone. The service went as usual until the hymn that followed the offering. When the second verse of "Victory in Jesus" says "And then I cried, Dear Jesus, come and heal my broken spirit", I began to cry. When the song was over, the guest pastor stood up, turned around, looked through the small congregation, until he seen me. When his eyes met mine, he quietly said, "I have a message from God for someone here. He says you have no need for a broken spirit. He has much better ahead for you." I couldn't breathe. Everyone in the room looked like they were frozen. When he sat down again, they began to move and look around uncomfortably. They knew something strange had happened but didn't know what.

After the service, I asked some of them if they had heard or felt something different– they said yes, "it was so strange" and couldn't figure out what had happened. I know that God wanted me – and only me - to hear that message. And, though the battle wasn't won, I now had joyful hope.

I went home to more fighting and misery, but I knew that somehow it would be okay. I grew up thinking that all marriages were male dominated and that wives were just not measuring up to what their husbands needed. That it was all about pleasing them and giving them everything they needed before they even asked for it. Love was earned. And, that I just needed to keep trying harder. I didn't have a clue as to what God was going to do. I didn't have a clue as to what I should do. But – He moved things along quickly. This was the beginning of Him taking the reins. Thank You my Lord!!! I LOVE YOU!!!!

I listed my house for sale and the divorce was filed. This was in the spring of '07 in the housing debacle. Things weren't selling, but I had three offers. All fell through within a few weeks of closing due to financing issues. The last offer tanked the morning of closing. The house had already been emptied.

I had planned to move to California to a family member who had asked. (Notice the "I had planned" Not God had planned….) I picked up a friend at the airport who was going to drive there with me. We stopped at a gas station to fill up, and I noticed behaviors that sent red flags flying everywhere in my head and heart. I prayed hard. "Dear heavenly Father, Lord, I need You now! Father, if this is going to be a disaster for me like everything else I have ever done- Please stop it now!" Four days later – that friend was dead. There are no words in any language to describe how afraid, lost, confused, and bewildered I was. I was in total shock. I went to California to pay respects to family members and returned home.

All my adult life, everyone assumed that I was leaving all these wonderful men because I got bored and was 'looking for greener pastures that didn't need mowing.' I never refuted any accusations or defended myself at all. It would have been too painful. Let everyone think what they will. That's what they'd do no matter what I would say. Again – People see what you do. God sees your heart. He knows why you did it. I hadn't had a lot of contact with my family for many years. I understand that I was an embarrassment to them and their families. How could they explain my life to those who asked how I was doing? I didn't want my messes to overshadow their lives.

But God used one of them in a big way at this point. She was very firm with me as she led me to where I had always wanted to be. "Dear Heavenly Father, please Lord, forgive me of all my sins. I am so sorry. Please lead me and guide me according to Your will, Your purposes and

Your plans. I need You. Father, You made me and You alone know how to fix my life. I will love You and serve You with all that I am for as long as I live. Please fill me with the presence of Your Holy Spirit. My life is Yours, in Jesus' precious name, amen.

Then we went through a workbook that drew me deep down into the heart of God. 2 Cor. 5:17 says "Therefore if any man be in Christ, he is a new creature; old things are passed away; behold, all things are become new." There is nothing so big and bad that He can't forgive. He will always give us a 'do over' if we ask. The consequences will remain. He doesn't erase them. I think that they serve as a reminder of who we were then as compared to who we are now.

And – if we are still tempted by the call of Satan, there is a verse for that! 1 Cor. 10:13. "The temptations in your life are no different from what others experience. AND God is faithful. He will not allow the temptation to be more than you can stand. When (not if…) you are tempted, He will show you a way out, so you can endure."

We have to want our hearts to change and then ask. Listen to 'the little voice in your head'. If a "funny little feeling" tells you something is wrong – listen to it. That is the Holy Spirit gently trying to guide you in the right direction. Don't do it. Walk away. Pray for strength to resist. He will help. He wants good things for us, not a ruined life of misery and regrets.

God started moving very quickly in my life. Just a few days later I knew that He wanted me to remove the house listing and sell it myself. I said "Lord, I don't know anything about selling a house. And the realtor is a friend". I heard "Do it anyway".

So – I did. I removed the listing and made flyers which were put up in every public place in several counties. Another friend helped me make a huge sign to place at the end of the driveway. A lot of people looked, but I was expecting it to sell in the first week. Every day when I would leave there, I would say, "Lord – why isn't this house selling??? Why do I have this thing hanging around my neck???"

One day as I was driving out, I stopped at the end of the driveway and said, "Lord! Thank You for this house! There are so many people who are so much worse off than I am. They would be so thankful to have a house to sell!! Father, I thank You for this. It is an asset, not a liability! Thank you, dear Lord!!!"

The next day, I had a call from a young man who wanted to see the house. He was already preapproved and loved the house! It was exactly what he wanted! We signed papers and I praised my Heavenly Father!

That weekend I went to church with a friend and thanked Him for the blessings I had received and the blessings yet to come. I prayed for guidance and direction as to what He wanted for my life. And where I would live and serve Him. When I got home, I made dinner for an elderly couple who were like second parents to me. I had been helping them daily for the past five or six years, driving to doctor appointments, cleaning, shopping, and meals, etc. I had been staying with them since I emptied out my house for the closing that fell through. When dinner was over, and they were comfortably settled in the living room, I did dishes, straightened up the kitchen a little, and picked up the local paper. I had never looked at these before, just threw them into the recycle bin. I picked it up and randomly opened it. The first thing that caught my eyes was an ad for a small home in a retirement community in a very southern state. And - it was extremely affordable. So, I called the local number. He answered and the first thing I asked was why it was for sale. He sadly said that his wife had passed away and his children didn't want him to go down there alone. We talked for a few more minutes and hung up. I prayed about it that night.

When I woke up in the morning, I thought "If God wants to give me a gift; I need to hold out open hands and take it!" So, I called him back and he said that he would be home after church and to come out and see pictures. I was happy and at peace. He went to church, so I knew that he must love the Lord. I felt that I could trust him.

I drove out to his home and spent a peaceful afternoon with a wonderful elderly man. He had been home builder, and then turned to cabinetry creation. His house was well done so I knew that he had been truthful about the home he was selling.

He asked what I had for furniture, etc. I said that I didn't have much of anything. I pretty much lost it all. He said "Praise God! After what you have been through (he knew the whole story through a mutual friend), I want you to drive down there and walk in. Everything is there. Fully furnished just as it was on the day I had to leave because my wife passed away. I want you to walk in, make a pot of coffee in *YOUR* coffee pot, sit down at *YOUR* table, and enjoy the peace. He wasn't kidding. It was walk-in ready and beautiful. He even had someone go in and clean and change the bed linens! And – this is how amazing God is – the price he was asking was a few dollars less than what the realtor's commission would have been! I headed south to a paid for house while driving a paid for vehicle with a positive bank balance!!!!

I have never done anything in this world to earn or deserve the mercy, grace, blessings, and provisions that He has given to me! He is a loving Father who wants to love and bless us, and sometimes, spoil us absolutely rotten! Oh, Father God – who am I that YOU would look down and notice me? Sinner that I am? I am so humbled by Your loving care.

Some interesting things happened before I left for my new home. The daughter of the couple whom I had been staying with thanked me for all that I had done for her parents. Then, she began asking a few borderline personal questions. I stopped her and said, "Do you happen to remember a big fat girl from school who wore a wig?" She stared at me for a very long moment and said "What???" I said "You know the one you used to chase?? She was in 7th grade, and you were in high school?" She turned very pale and stared at me again, slowly connecting the dots. Tears flowed.

Finally, she said "Oh no… My granddaughters are being bullied so badly in their school and I used to do that to you. I am so sorry. I am getting back what I gave. Can you ever forgive me??" I told her that I had forgiven her as soon as she had done it and was very sorry that her little ones were suffering. To this day, I pray for them all. I think there was closure on a chapter there for both of us.

A second one was when people began asking where I was moving to. They asked, "How did you find out that it was for sale?" I told them, and they said that they always read that paper looking for that sort of opportunity. I asked the seller how many calls he had received. He said, "None until my deal with you was signed." I believe that God hid it from others to save it for me.

What a sad and joyful thing to head south. I would miss many people, parents, 'second' parents, grandkids, and many friends. But God was calling, and I was answering. I drove through a blizzard midway, and not realizing that entrance accesses to rest areas weren't plowed yet, I hit the first one at full speed. By the grace of God, I kept my truck between the ditches and came to a sliding stop right in front of the door. I got out and calmly walked in only to be met by four laughing men.

I looked at them and said "So – who won the bet?" The guy leaning on the broom raised his hand. He said "I seen your plates from way up north and knew you could handle that thing. I gave him a high five and looked at the rest and said, "You had little faith!" They were still laughing when I left.

It has always been a great source of wonder for me how the world changes as one travels. Snowbanks turn into palm trees! Praise God! The plants that we painstakingly grow indoors in the north grow like wildfire outside in the south. And it was so good to see cattle grazing on green grass in the winter.

I stopped at a visitor center about fifty miles north of my new home. When I walked in, the lady asked if she could help me. I said "Yes, I want to sit down on something that is not moving at a high rate of speed!" She laughed and asked what brought me there. I gave her the address of my new house and asked her where it was. She looked at me like I had lost my mind! She said, "You bought a house that you have never seen????" I said "Yes, I did. God brought me here."

She gave me great directions and I was on my way! I had never even bought a map. I knew that if I headed south, there would be signs and God would lead me in. And He did! I remember turning in and seeing rows of palm trees and red hibiscus, jasmine, and so many other beautiful plants and flowers. The soft ocean breezes and the flowers smelled delightful! I turned and there was my house. I got out and walked into the most amazing peace I have ever known. Everything was there. I needed nothing except a few perishable groceries.

A new neighbor walked by and introduced herself and lent me her gate opener, so I could go get the things I needed. Everyone was so sweet and friendly. I finally for the first time in my life had total complete sweet peace in my Lord. I was exactly where I wanted to be. For the first time – I was home – in His will. Another neighbor and his wife invited me to go with them to church and I was thrilled. All the way down, I had prayed for a church. "Lord, if it is half as good as my sister's church, I will be so happy." Well – this church flat rocked! It was amazing! (Except that the Pastor was wrong about the barn thing!!)

I arrived at the end of November and flew to my daughter's home for Christmas. I had a great time with her and my grandchildren. I flew home on New Year's Eve Day. It was so warm and beautiful; I was in love with my new home. But I soon discovered that God had a reason for my being there. He had sent me on a mission.

After I had unpacked my suitcase, I decided to go for a walk through the retirement community. Everyone was out enjoying the warm weather and was so friendly. It was more than I could ever have imagined. I watched a large motor home pull in through the gate. I assumed that they had enjoyed Christmas at home before heading south for the coldest months. I said a quiet prayer thanking God for their safe arrival and that they would be blessed there. That was on a Monday.

Every Thursday morning, there was a 'coffee and donuts' time at the community center. All were encouraged to attend. So, I was taken and introduced by my new friend. Being very shy, it was uncomfortable to stand up, introduce myself and tell everyone where I came from.... I escaped at the first opportunity. I just kind of slid out the side door.... Took a deep breath of fresh flowery air and praised God for the easy way out. Only to look forward and see a man standing there like he was waiting for me.

*Dear Lord. NO. I am allergic. I will break out in spots. I have been set free. Go away. Now.*

"Can I ask you a question?"

*Ok. Be polite. What would Jesus do?* So, I said, "Yes, but I probably don't have an answer." That was a true statement. He asked if someone would be more likely to take his dad to get groceries if he had his own car or would they want to drive their own. I must have looked really dense to him because I just stared at him. He explained that he had driven his elderly father down in the motor home and was leaving as soon as he was settled in.

The man was in his eighties and would be alone unable to drive or anything else. So, true to my nature, I said that I might be able to take him. I couldn't see anyone being alone with no help. Then he asked, "Is anyone here born again?" I told him that I was. He was so happy! He said, "Where do you live?" I said, "Over there", as I was waving my arm in random directions. He said that he had to go check on his dad. Great idea. And I made a hasty retreat.

I walked in the house and started to make some coffee that I could enjoy in peace. I never thought to lock the door.... I filled the pot with water; put the filter in and there was a knock at the door. Before I could get there or inquire, the door popped open. And there he stood.

"Thought this was where you went…. Cute little place you have here…. Oh good… coffee…. You sit down and let me finish this up for you…."

*OK LORD…. What is happening here?? Could You please remove this man from my house????* And he kept talking like he had known me all his life. I was sitting there staring at him like I was just transported to another planet. *OK LORD…. HELP!!!! SOS…. HELLOOOOO???*

He talked for a while about his dad. I finally said that I would meet him and maybe I could take him for groceries and doctor's appointments…. So, I walked with him and met his dad. He was a sweet, funny WWII veteran who really did need help. His dad wanted his own car because he didn't want me to put miles on my vehicle. Since I was going to be the designated driver, I was drafted to help pick out this car. And that involved a few days of searching and lunches…

And then came the day that he said that he really liked me. *No. You can't like me. I gave my life to the Lord. And I have a past. You have no idea. You don't even know me. I don't know you…. We just met… He kept pushing. Go away….* I told him everything. I have always told the truth. Some things one can't hide in a relationship. It will all come out. That didn't scare him at all. I thought for sure he would run for the hills. But I didn't know that God had this all worked out. He was an amazing man, Army 173rd Airborne Viet Nam veteran, still working. A tall, strong, handsome cross between John the Baptist and Johnny Cash, he was a commanding presence. God used him to quickly pull me so very far down deep into the heart of obedience and prayer. I knew where he thought we were heading. I was terrified of being out of God's will.

One day, I went into the bathroom (my substitute prayer closet) on my knees – face to the floor – and cried out to God. I was crying so hard telling Him that I didn't understand this at all. "You brought me down here and set me free from all this stuff, so I can serve you. How can this be Your will???? Lord- Please!! I need to know for sure what You want me to do! I don't ever want to be out of Your will again. I don't want to do this!!! Please Lord – tell me!!!" I finally got up and stood there totally empty – absolutely drained. I stood staring at the mascara which was running all over my face and was too worn out to fix it. Suddenly, I heard a deep voice, with words spoken as clearly as any I have ever heard. *"I HAVE PROVIDED FOR YOU."* I stood there and took it all in. Wow…. God provides Christians spouses! I said "Thank You my Lord. And, yes, I will marry him."

He came to visit again in February, just before Valentine's Day. I thought nothing of it because I am not the kind of woman that men go all out for on holidays. For me, it had always been just another day. No big deal. Well…. this time, there was a knock on the door as soon as I raised my blinds to indicate that I was up, and devotions were done. (He later told me that he had been out walking, waiting for me to get up since 4:30 a.m.)

There he stood holding a huge vase of red roses. I was speechless! He brought them in, arranged them to perfection and proceeded to make me breakfast. I can promise you - this was definitely a first in my world! I said, "What am I supposed to do???" He said, "You just sit there and look pretty." I nearly passed out. Words like those had never been aimed at me. I thought that he may have vision issues – but *Lord – please don't fix them now!!*

That evening, he took me to dinner at Olive Garden. I really almost did pass out there! On one knee – in front of the entire packed, cheering, and clapping crowd - this man slipped a beautiful ring on my finger and proposed to me! And, I tearfully accepted! We set the date for March 14th.

Everyone thought I was crazy. They were criticizing and condemning me for 'going back to my old ways', 'I thought you were born again'… 'like a dog going back to its vomit…' I heard it all. But – I had peace – most days. I was still walking in prayer. If it wasn't His will, He sure knew that I would follow His lead. But – He kept pushing me forward.

We were married, and life moved on. He went back and forth from his work to me. It was going very well. I felt loved and appreciated for the first time ever! He told me that I was the wife he had always dreamed of, and I had a husband that I never thought I would have. I took him to my Bible study one night. It was always over before eight p.m. This evening, my friends were asking questions that had never been answered. They sat spell bound as he answered, explained, and taught. He would tell me the scriptures and I would quickly look them up and read them. He knew the Bible so well. We didn't leave until almost midnight.

Recently one of the ladies told me that when she remembers that night, she still gets emotional. "It was like we were in the presence of something indescribable!" I agreed. The Holy Spirit was there with us. I thank God for that night.

Three months after our marriage, he was diagnosed with bone cancer from his contact with Agent Orange in Vietnam. Two months, two days from diagnosis to death. I stayed with him while he was hospitalized twice – never left his side. Meds every two hours – 24-7. On my knees. Praying for healing. He said, "You be very careful when you pray. ALWAYS pray 'according to His will.' Not what you want." His faith never failed, wavered, or slowed in any way.

Before I married him, I prayed, "Lord, if I am to marry this man, I pray that You will give me what I need to be his wife. I know that I don't have it, whatever it is. Please fill me with Your blessings Lord, I need You." It didn't take long until I realized what He had given me. I am the squeamish one who faints at the sight of blood coming out of someone else (mine – I can deal with), and I can't stand to see or hear someone throw up – I throw up.

One morning, I had to remove the surgical staples out of his incisions and then after he ate lunch, he threw it all up. I laid down my sandwich, ran and changed his clothes, cleaned him up, and made him comfortable again. I walked back into the kitchen, washed my hands and sat down at the table. I picked up my sandwich again and began to eat. Then- it hit me! I didn't throw up. I didn't even feel nauseous!!! Praise God!!! That was what I would need and didn't have! He knew, and He provided! He knows us all better than we know ourselves.

All through this short and yet seemingly long time, I was blessed with amazing friends who supported and loved me through it all. One would call at what would normally be very strange times. But it was always exactly when I needed to hear his soft, gentle, encouraging voice the most. His beautiful wife's timing was perfect in her own way. She called when all was peaceful and quiet, and I had the time to relax and smile for a few minutes. God used them when I needed them. His children were amazing and supportive. I was very blessed to know them. His best friend from childhood walked beside me from beginning to end. He came many miles and stayed in motels for weeks just to be there for both of us. As did his beloved sister – who I love and respect dearly! There were many who helped, and we were greatly blessed through the whole journey. When we have to 'walk through the fire', we don't walk alone. God is always with us and He provides others to walk beside us.

My pastor gave me a short piece of nylon rope with a hole drilled through it during this time. I asked what it was. He said that it was to remind me that sometimes – in the physical world - that I was all someone had to hold onto. I still have it on my key ring.

I clearly remember the moment when the hospice nurse looked at me and said, "He has 1 week left." I said, "For what?" She said, "To live." I was stunned. How did she know? She wasn't God. She was wrong. And - I told her she was wrong. "Thank you for coming", in an 'and there's the door…' attitude. But- she was right. To the day. But I didn't know it or accept it. One day after she had given me the bad forecast, my husband somehow found the strength to pull up, and play Johnny Cash and June Carter's song, "Far side Banks of Jordan" for me. I cried for a long time. He said, "Woman, don't ever forget this." To this day, I still cry every time I hear it.

The night before he passed, I knelt and prayed, "Lord, I thank You for my precious husband. I am so blessed to have him! I pray Father, that if it is Your will, that You would heal him. But Lord if it isn't, I pray that You will take him home and Jesus – hold him tight until I get there." His son was with us and he asked me if I would like to lie beside him that night. I was uncertain why he had asked me that, but I said that I would. I laid down beside him carefully, put one arm around him and held his hand in my other one. I prayed again with him. He hadn't opened his eyes for a few hours, but I knew he could hear me. When I was done, I told him how much I loved him, and how amazing he was. And, then I said, "And- by the way you are still the handsomest man in the state!" He smiled as he squeezed my hand and I saw him roll his eyes under closed lids! That's my sweetheart! I awakened at 1:14 a.m. when he took his last breath. Five months and gone. He died on our fifth month anniversary. When he was diagnosed, we said that we would celebrate each month like it was a year because we didn't know how much time we would have. We never imagined that it would be only five months.

It was hard to believe that he was gone. But as I thought about it, I was humbled beyond words. God knew that he had the cancer. And out of all the single, born-again women in this world, He chose ME to walk through this with him. ME. He trusted ME with this unbelievable amazing man's care – to love him through it. That is why He moved me there so quickly. I saw all the puzzle pieces fitting smoothly together. Wow! Thank You my Lord for Your trust in me to do Your will.

After life settled into a new kind of normal, I had to have a second neck surgery. He and I had been rear ended at a stoplight on our way home from church our first Sunday together. That was my seventh car accident.... The eighth was another "stopped at a red light and hit incident" .... Out of eight accidents – none "at fault", four were at stoplights or signs. Three were at about 10-15 mph when hit. Perhaps my younger flying low days made me a harder target to hit...... ;-).

By the following spring, I was getting back on my feet, and spent the entire summer with family and grandkids. What an amazing time! I loved playing with cute little boys and enjoyed hanging laundry on a clothesline, watching a garden grow, and roasting hotdogs and marshmallows over a campfire at night.

One day, I was with the boys at the park and I was watching them slide down the slide and play, and it was so joyful to see the little boys playing and having so much fun running around in a sandbox, playing on merry- go- rounds and swings. While watching them, I was on the phone with my little sister. I was in tears. I told her, "It is so wonderful to watch my grandsons play." She said, "Think about it ... This is how God feels when He looks down watching His children enjoying the life he planned for them."

It really doesn't get much better than that. Sundays were spent at a small church being fed from the Word, then going to visit my parents in the afternoon. The time went way too quickly. Again – those are precious memories. In the fall, I headed for home.

It was so good to be home in my own peaceful quiet little house again. I felt the same peace all over again that I felt the first time I saw it. It was such a sweet, calm, serene peace. I spent a lot of time in reading His word, and in prayer. I was having some health issues and by May, I needed a third neck surgery, and I was diagnosed with pancreatic cancer. My 'gastrin' level was 1,117. The doctor said that it was extremely high. *Ok Lord.... What's up with this???*

The surgeon who would do the neck surgery was in a larger city 5-6 hours away. I had no one to drive me there and back. Plus, I couldn't drive for six weeks after that.

I was trying to figure out the logistics on this one when I got the second report. My doctor said that the two best places that she could send me was a clinic in Minnesota or one in Texas. *Ok Lord…. I don't know what You are doing, but I need help.*

When a friend called that afternoon, I told him what was happening. He said, "Well, this is easy. We know all about one, having had family members there before. I can fly down and drive you back up here after your neck surgery and show you the ropes at the clinic. But – there is a stop that we must make on the way back.

"I am registered to attend a Vietnam veteran's reunion following your surgery and we have to go."

*"Oh no Lord. I am not going to one of those. I can't bear this. Too many memories. Lord – this just can't be Your will."* So, I called a pastor friend whom I have known since high school. When I told him the situation, he said that he would be in prayer with me about it, but had I ever considered 'putting out a fleece' as Gideon did in Judges 6:37-40. So, I prayed before I went to bed, "…. And Lord, please send me a sign. I need to know that this is Your will. This seems so strange and awkward to me."

Very early the next morning I received a phone call from the friend of a friend stating that whatever I was going to do, I needed to do it. Ok. Well, by 4:30 p.m., I did what Gideon did. I asked God for another sign. I put my husband's wedding ring in my pocket and said "Lord, if I am to go do this, I will take this to a pawn shop and if they give me $50.00 for it, I know that I should go. If it is less, I will know that I should not go. This was tearing at my heart as I quickly got into the car before I could change my mind.

I walked into the corner store with my heart in my throat. When a young man asked if he could help me, I laid it on the counter and asked him if they bought things like this. He asked, "How much do you want for it?" I said, "Oh no. You tell me." So, he picked it up and weighed it. He took it into the back and talked to fellow employees about it.

After what seemed like a very long time, he came back out and had a small piece of paper on the palm of his hand. He laid it down with his hand over it. He looked at me and said "Ready?" *As ready as I'll ever be, I guess….* He moved his hand and it said $200.00! I started to cry. He felt so bad and said," You don't have to sell it!!!" I said, "You don't understand. I made a deal with God, I can't go back." I went home, called my friends and plans were made.

All went well with the surgery, and we were on our way north. I was a wee bit crabby because I hate neck braces even though I know that they are essential to a positive surgical outcome. I was cranky, irritated, and trying to figure out what God was doing. He keeps us on an "as we need to know" basis. And I was born with an over active curiosity factor. But no matter how I turned this situation – I could make no sense of it at all. So, I had to apologize to Him and to those He chose to use in my life. God can and will use anyone – believer or not to help and bless others. They just don't realize it. And sometimes they don't want to know….

Fast forward…. I am at a hotel I don't want to be in…. wearing a neck brace that I wish I could throw out the window at about 75 mph…. listening to conversations about a war that I wish had never existed…… hearing stories about comrades who now had cancer or some other war related issue or had died…… trying to be somewhat friendly and pleasant to really nice people when I just wanted to go home and not hurt anymore.

On the second day of the reunion, a group of us were walking back from a nearby restaurant when I noticed a man in a power wheelchair heading across the parking lot. He was heading straight to me. So, I just stood there and waited. He was wearing a goofy hat that made me smile, so I commented on it. We stayed there and talked for a while. I asked him to pray for me as I was having some health issues. He said that he would, as a woman appeared at the door calling for him to come in to dinner. Thank You Lord. He gave me his email address and asked me to let him know how it all turned out.

Later that night, one of my friends said, "When you 'born again' people meet, it's like no one else exists." I apologized. I tried to explain that it is like meeting a long-lost family member. We have a lot in common. There is a special bond. This man was calm, very peaceful, and had a good sense of humor.

I prayed that night "Lord, if You would ever want me to walk beside a man like that, I would love him, honor him, and protect him with everything in me for as long as I live." This one was married I assumed, because only a wife would let him know that he was late for dinner like that. (I kind of figured that I was safe….) He didn't let the wheelchair thing get him down at all. He had one of the most positive attitudes that I had ever seen. I was really asking God for forgiveness about my bad attitude. I could still walk and do pretty much everything I wanted to. That was the end of crabby me.

So, I had made it through the reunion, met new people, and was grateful for many things. And on to my clinic appointments. It is an amazing place. It was huge, and full of hurting people seeking the best medical answers. I had round one of tests and went back and forth from friends' homes to nearby family member's homes. After one series, I emailed the 'wheelchair man' and asked if he made it home ok. I never received a reply. I had sent another one a week or so later – still no reply. *Ok. All must be well… Thank You Lord.*

The test results would come in and they would be "not good, we need you back for more tests". So, there were several more trips. On probably the third return trip, I was packed and had everything in the car except my laptop. I came back in to grab it and say goodbye. I wrapped the cord, closed the top, and put it in the case – zipped it up. I picked it up, took two steps across the kitchen door and I heard a voice say, "Email him." I said "Nope. Already did that. No answer." And I took another step. "Email him now." I said, "I did. Twice. He didn't answer me." And I took another step. "NOW." And Father, forgive me; I said "WHATEVER." And I think I rolled my eyes –at God. Lord- I am soooo sorry!!!!

I pulled out the computer, turned it on and hit 'email'. I sent something like "Well, hope all is well and you're still alive…" and hit 'send'. Immediately, a reply came back. It was long. I know he couldn't type that fast. There is no earthly way that could have happened. It was a long email. He was ok. No troubles getting home. All was well except that the mother board on his computer had fried. He had to get a new one. Someone had to bring it and install it. He had lost my email address. He was so very happy to hear from me…… *Oh boy….*

After a week or so of emails, I was informed that he was not married. The lady was his sister. I informed him that I had lost a husband two years prior. (We had met on his birthday.) I didn't want to go through anything like that again. Ever. Then he asked if he could call me. "I would much rather talk than type" he said. I was thinking *"I'm sure you would…. Ok, now what Lord?"* So, I gave him my number and we talked for hours every day.

I recall the final 'test' at the clinic was having my stomach pumped to retrieve stomach acids, or whatever was down there. If you have been blessed with never having to go through this procedure, I highly recommend staying on that route. It is nasty. Worse than giving birth – by far. As she was pushing this tube (which felt like a large 50' garden hose….) down my throat – saying "swallow…. swallow" … I was trying to breathe, not throw up, not choke to death, etc. This was horrid. And – joy of all joys – this delightful pumping procedure was going to last an entire hour.

There were many jars lined up on the counter waiting to be filled. I laid there for about the longest ten minutes of my life when I began to panic. I prayed, *"Lord, I can't do this. If I have to get through this, I need Your help!"* Instantly, I felt like a small child, picked up by a loving Daddy, held tightly, and snuggled down into His shoulder. I fell asleep in His arms. I felt no discomfort at all.

The next thing I remember was the nurse telling me it was over. I was to take a deep breath and she gave the tube a quick yank and the whole thing came out! (Good thing I didn't know how to get it out earlier….) There was approximately a quarter of a cup of stomach acid in the jar. That was all. She was very surprised. She said that usually there are many full jars and sometimes she had run out of empties. Whatever the outcome – thank You Lord – this is over!!!

Later that afternoon, I went to my doctor's office for results. When I walked in, she asked how I was. A wee bit sarcastically, I answered, "Absolutely wonderful, that's why I am here…." She smiled and said she knew that it hadn't been pleasant. Father, please forgive my mouth…. She hesitantly said, "Well - actually – you are fine." As she showed me the results, she explained the numbers and there was no indication of cancer anywhere now. She quietly said, "It isn't what we expected." I asked," What were you expecting?" As she struggled for words, I asked "Cancer?" She reluctantly said that probably, yes. I said, "God healed me." Her eyes opened wide in surprise, and she said, "Yes, He must have!"

I still had a serious health issue that I had lived with all my life that couldn't be dealt with anywhere. I had always been very anemic. As my Grandmother had been. She somehow managed to swallow two tablespoons of the nastiest tasting "blackstrap molasses" every day because it was high in iron. Just the smell of that would head me out the door. This world famous clinic wouldn't allow treatment for it because I didn't test positive for Celiac disease. It didn't recognize "gluten intolerance" then. But, years later, they now do. My doctor and I had become quite close, and she hugged me and in tears, said, "I am afraid that you are going to die. Your iron levels are getting way too low. Your bone marrow is slowing down the making of red blood cells." I told her that I was in God's hands, and His will be done. I asked her to pray for me, and I would pray for her. And I still do today.

I thanked her for her work and joyfully left! Life is great, and God is amazing! I threw the neck brace into the relic pile and got on with life! I called my friends who walked through the past few years with me and told them first. They rejoiced with me, and we all thanked God! Since I was leaving for home the next day, I took my friend who had walked beside me through this chapter of life out to supper. We had a great time, and I was so overjoyed at the load of worry and fear that God had removed from my life and now, hope for a future, that on the way home, I became a little bit "lead footed" and took the exit ramp probably on two wheels…. My friend had wanted to listen to a radio station that I couldn't stand, so I was switching stations when I came across a country music station that was playing "I'm a brand-new man". I cranked it up and sang, "I'm a brand new gal" because God had just given me a new lease on life. My friend was rolling his eyes and making some negative noises when he looked in his side mirror…. And he said, "You have company. Pull over!" I looked, and lo and behold, there were definitely squad car lights behind me…. So, I pulled over. The State Patrol officer came to the window and asked, "Do you have any idea how fast you were going???" "NOPE" "DID you even see me???" "NOPE" "What were you doing???" "Well, I was just released from the hospital and God healed my cancer! No sign of it at all! So, I took my friend out to dinner before I head home tomorrow. And he doesn't like country music, so I turned it up loud and was singing and praising God!"

He said, "What do you mean 'he doesn't like country music'? What does he like???" I told him, and the officer looked in past me at my friend and said, "That isn't even music!" I said, "That's what I was trying to tell him, but he doesn't believe me!" He shook his head in unbelief. Then he said, "Is this car registered in your name?" "Yes" "Bring the title, registration, and insurance cards and get into my car."

Once I got into his squad car, he started asking me more questions. One was, "Why didn't you stop for the stop sign? Didn't you see it?" "Yes, I seen it, and I could see almost half a mile in each direction, and nothing was coming." "Yes, I did see you look." We talked a bit more, and he was a very nice young man at the end of his shift. He was happy for me, and thankful as well. He said that if I left town early in the morning and didn't get stopped again for anything at all in that state, he would just give me a warning ticket. I thanked him profusely as I promised I'd be careful and head out very early. I asked him how fast he had clocked me, but he couldn't tell me because then he'd have to write it up. So, I really didn't need to know at all!

Then I notified everyone else that I was cleared for takeoff and on the runway revving up! I was going home to my peaceful little house and thank Him forever and I was never going to leave again!!!! My new friend in the wheelchair wanted me to drive there so he could join me for a celebration dinner. But that was a long way in an opposite direction...... I declined and headed home. But God had another plan.

I arrived home and took a huge deep breath of relief. Such sweet peace lived in that house. I had never felt so at home anywhere in my adult life as I did in that house. I thanked God for bringing me home safely and strong.

It wasn't long before I began to feel a strange emptiness that I had never felt before in my life. I could not understand it at all. I had a full, very blessed life. God was putting this 'emptiness' in me for a reason. I just didn't know it then. (One day I even said, "Lord, I'm bored!" He must have smiled!)

I was still talking to my new friend a lot. He had found out that he had to go to a very large city with very heavy traffic in a neighboring state for a doctor's appointment. He was understandably concerned and afraid. I asked if there was someone from his church who would go with him. I finally did volunteer to drive up, but someone else went with him.

Then came a second appointment and I again reluctantly volunteered. This time, he accepted. I prayed hard, "Dear Lord, is this Your will? Do you want me to go???" I didn't get a "NO, stay home", so I packed and headed out. About four hours from home, I said "Lord – You have made such an amazing place for us to live! This is beautiful! You know I love a good road trip. Now, can I go home?" "No." Ok. So, I drove on taking the long scenic route. I found a hotel for the night and thanked Him for the trip, His provision, and plan – whatever it was…. Slept well and arose, prayed, and left.

Again, I drove through a part of America that I had never seen. This is a huge country with an amazing array of landscapes and climates. I stopped in the afternoon for gas, and said, "Ok Lord – this has been a really nice ride. Can I go home now?" "NO." Ok. And away I went again. The last time I asked was when I crossed into his state. I said, "Ok Lord. It's still not too late. If You want me to, I can still go home…." "NO." So, on I went.

If you have ever tried to disengage a cat from sheer window curtains, you will have a better understanding of what our Lord goes through with me. You hold said cat carefully so there is no more damage.

You carefully extricate each claw gently and carefully. Sometimes this requires help because as you get one paw free, it automatically wants to fly back into the curtain. Plus, most cats really liked hanging from the curtain in the first place …. Father- please forgive me!

I pulled into his driveway and thought, *well, there must be a reason He brought me here and I'm about to find out.* We talked outside and in the garage for a while before we went into the house.

That's when God had to keep His hands firmly on me. I wanted to run! Fast! To the car. Reverse. Home. High rate of speed. Then I thought another minute and realized that if I did, I would have to take him with me. There was no way that I could have left him there. I have never seen a house in such a mess. It was all I could do to stay there that night. I asked him if there was a motel nearby. God said, "Stay." So, I did. It wasn't easy…

First thing – lock the non-house broken dog out of all carpeted areas. Unload a recliner so I had a place to sleep and pray for guidance (and deliverance???).

Early the next morning, I tackled cleaning the kitchen. It took all day to clean the stove and sink so I could do dishes. There are no words to describe how He got me through this. I spent three very long days there before we headed to his appointment.

He had to attend classes to learn how to drive with hand controls. On the way down, he said, "It is so strange. I feel like there is a ring on my finger" while rubbing his left ring finger. And, God's cat in the curtain thought, "I don't think so." The driving lessons didn't go well. The Agent Orange connected MS had done too much damage to his motor control. He couldn't drive any more.

God knows what lies ahead of us and He plans for us according to our needs. He knew that this sweet precious peaceful man would be in serious trouble soon, so He sent me. Again – Lord, there must be many born again single women. And You chose me. I am humbled and awestruck beyond belief. There was absolutely no way that I would have ever met him had God not intervened. We were well over a thousand miles apart. He couldn't drive that far, and I would never just randomly travel there. He had told me that if I would come up to help him, that when the appointment was over, he would take me on a tour of his part of the country.

So, we went on a tour of God's beautiful land. I had never explored that much of the west. I enjoyed it and the history. After seeing the mountains and the deserts, I realized that if people like me had been born back in pioneer history, the west would have never been settled. It must have taken an amazing amount of faith and courage! I would have stayed well east of the Mississippi!!! But – then again – God has a way of getting me moving, so who knows….

All I know is that our ancestors had more courage and perseverance than I do. And, they got all the way west without a decent map, GPS, hotels or even "porta-potties"…. Thank You Lord that I was born where and when I was. I would have loved being a pioneer where I grew up, but I greatly appreciate the blessings that we have now.

Somewhere towards the end of that journey, I was reloading luggage into the van when he stopped me and said, "Can I ask you a question?" Automatically, I thought *"Oh no – now what did I do wrong???"* All the alarm bells from the past went off. Usually that question was asked right before I was yelled at, or the violence began…. I said "Now what did I do? Have I forgotten something?" He quietly said, "No. I love you. Will you marry me?" And I tearfully and joyfully again, said "YES!!!!" We spent a couple more days exploring before we went back to his house to break the news to his family.

Again, all the "You don't even know each other" …... comments flew up. But we had spent months talking on the phone for 2-6 hours a day. We knew each other very well. The pastor who married us said that in all the years of ministry and marriages, we knew each other better than any other couple had. He said that I knew him very well and how he would react to things more than anyone else they had ever counseled. I said, "I guess that's why God put us together."

One of his doubting family members came to visit one day and looked me straight in the eyes and said," Do you know that you are the squeakiest clean person I have ever known? Except for all those marriages, you don't even have a speeding ticket! Do you know that I paid the 'big bucks' and nothing turned up???" (So…. If you pay more for these things, are you supposed to find more dirt?? I don't understand….) When I could finally speak, I said, "And were you surprised? What did you expect or hope to find?" No answer….

That surprised me, but a few days later, I asked her to stand up with me since my daughter couldn't come. (When my daughter did meet him a few weeks later, she gave him a hug and said, "It is so good to meet you. Welcome to the family. You are now the only baby chicken with the world's worst mother hen. Good luck with that!" And they both laughed!!!)

A couple years later, that lady asked me to forgive her for running a background check on me. I said, "I have nothing to forgive you for. It wasn't me that you didn't trust. It was God that you didn't trust. That is between you and Him. We're good." FYI – don't look now… I do have a speeding ticket…. I got caught in a locally famous speed trap in a small town during their rodeo weekend radar traps…. On the brakes but didn't get it down to 35 in time…. I think of all the times I could have had one and then got this one for 'barely' speeding…. It happened on a day when I was helping someone, whom I felt that God had specifically told me not to help previously, because "they are leaning on you and not me." And I did it anyway. That was the last time for that. He chastises the ones He loves. Thank You Lord for loving me enough to stop me from doing things that are not pleasing to You.

I spent the fall cleaning his house and restoring a home for him. Chaos was removed, and peace moved in. By the winter, things were better for him, and I too had peace with God's plans. I have had many people tell me that they "will get right with the big man upstairs right before they die" and that they don't want to live a "boring Christian life". Two things on that… 1. You may be killed instantly and have no time to do anything. And 2. It sure isn't boring. I can hardly keep up. Life has never been so blessed, exciting and amazing. The regrets that I do have are because of wasted minutes, days, months, and years of my life that were lived out of His will and how many blessings and joys I must have missed. Now I know why I felt empty and lost my whole entire life. A group of family and friends were talking a few months ago when I said that I loved the Smoky Mountains and would love to have a cabin there. A beautiful young lady asked me why I had to wait for God to send me there. Why didn't I just go there on my own?

This question had just sprung forth from a sweet lady who had quit a job she loved, moved to a city that she dislikes, hours away from her loved ones, to take a job that she hates, living in a small 'crummy' apartment that she hates with a girl that she doesn't really get along with well….

Honey, I think the answer should be painfully obvious. I don't want to be there. Been there – done that. Not going back. He knows if it will work out and if I will be happy. The world is full of problems. He doesn't promise that we will be problem free. But He does promise that He will walk through them with us. "If God leads you to it, He will bring you through it."

If we get ourselves into a mess on our own, He can get us out if we ask for forgiveness and help, but we still must deal with the consequences. I am well over 60. I don't want any more of the above.

We were married on what would have been my grandparents ninety third anniversary, closed up his house for the winter and headed into the sunny south. I much prefer flip-flops to mukluks. It seemed like I no more unpacked the van before I had to repack and head back north. I don't know how the 'snowbirds' do it. It is a lot of work, and way too much packing for me. We talked about it as we were getting his house redone. It needed everything, all flooring replaced, walls repaired and repainted, new interior doors and woodwork, basically a floor to ceiling renovation.

In the middle of the summer, he decided to sell the house when it was done. Simplify our lives! Sweet relief. When it was finished, he called a realtor. Everyone said that it would never sell. "You might want to think about renting it". "There are houses in this area that have been on the market for many years." "You might want to think about a 'rent to own' or a land contract." God had another plan. And- His plans always work. The realtor left the house at 1:30. She called at 2:00 and asked if she could show it at 4:00. "Sure!" So, we left.

The realtor was showing the house to a young couple who had looked at houses for four years. Everything either was too high priced or needed too much work. They had decided a few days before that they 'would look at one more house.' If they didn't like that one last house, they would stay where they were for a few more years and save up more money before they looked again. I heard that and thought "I wouldn't have four years of patience for that!" God bless those sweet kids! But…. God kept them from buying earlier because He knew that we would be selling that house. And that house would be perfect for them. He put it in their hearts to 'look at one more house'. They loved it and put in the offer which was joyfully accepted. We were all happy. That is what our loving heavenly Father really wants – our love and happiness. His timing is perfect. Always!

The summer of house renovations had another very interesting adventure. One day I had to take my husband to a doctor's appointment over one hundred miles away. This was across some rather barren land. One could drive for a long time without seeing another car depending on the day. I got him safely over there and safely home. Praise God! The next day I told him that we needed an oil change on the van and asked if he wanted to come with me. It was only about a year old. He said that he would rather stay home. So, I had the lube, oil, and filter done, and headed to the local building materials store for more paint and miscellaneous items.

I hadn't gone but a mile or so when I smelled something funny. I thought *"When I used to do this myself, sometimes I would spill a few drops of oil onto the engine, and it would have to smoke off. But now, they use a gas pump type handle so there should be no spillage…."* It quickly got worse, and all the dash lights lit up like a Christmas tree and the door locks all went crazy, as the van filled up with horrible smelling smoke. The doors wouldn't open. I prayed for God's protection and drove to the nearest store and parked in front of the first fire hydrant I saw. Suddenly, my door opened, and I got out quickly. The smoke was so thick inside that it was coming out around the windows and door seals. A brave young man helped me get my things out of there and the fire department was on its way. They disconnected the battery and towed it away.

My brother-in-law came to get me, and I was very happy to see him. I believe that God knew this was going to happen and held it off until I was alone. Had this happened out on the road in the middle of nowhere the previous day, I probably would never have been able to get my husband out. There was a hand crank for the ramp, but the side door wouldn't open so I couldn't have reached it or the place to insert it. And, with a very long response time, the battery wouldn't have been disconnected that soon and the van may have gone up like the fourth of July. If the doors had opened, I may not have been able to get us a safe distance from the vehicle.

The dealership or the manufacturing company never did figure out how to get that side door to open. They just bought it back from us. Thank You Lord, for protecting my husband.

It was winter again before we found a replacement lift equipped van and headed south. I look back at what I thought were 'trials' and in retrospect, they turned out to be amazing blessings. I met many of His precious people and he has moved us again.

By spring my anemia issue was accelerating, and no doctor at any healthcare facility would touch it at all. I had been to many cities, and many clinics and hospitals, in many states. I heard, "We've never seen or heard of anything like this." "No insurance will cover it." "There are no previous records of symptoms like yours, or proper treatment protocols."

I was told. "Your bone marrow has quit making red blood cells. You have six months to live."

So, again God intervened. My daughter had moved and wanted me to come up and repaint her new house, since the interior was all white. My husband had a doctor's appointment two hours north of us, he said, "Let's just head up from there." "Ok…" Once we got there, I painted and decorated every room for her. It was beautiful and now, felt like her home. After we had spent a week with her and my grandchildren, he said, "I like it here. Let's move up here…." Oh brother…. Another "pack and move". I was so sick of cardboard boxes and packing tape that I could still smell them in my sleep…. We looked, he found a house he liked, and wanted to put in an offer. Then, again, we drove another long trip home. "Lord, please help me. I need to know if this is Your will…." So, again, I did the Gideon Fleece thing. "Lord, if this is Your will, I will know it by Your sending a born-again Pastor who will have services here in this beautiful retirement park." And… God does have a sense of humor and precise timing. When I lifted my head, there was a truck pulling up to the door. And I knew the truck and I knew the people. A sweet lady who had been a widow for quite a few years had recently married a retired pastor whose wife had passed a few years before from cancer. Both sweet, a match made in Heaven. I walked to the door, and said, "Come on in. I've been waiting for you." They laughed and said, "Are you selling this house?" "Yes, but I just got done telling God that I wouldn't sell it to anyone except a pastor who would have services here." He laughed and said, "Nothing like putting God in a box!" I said, "No, I just wanted to be sure it is His will." He said, "I understand, when do you want to close on this?" "As soon as possible." So, off to Walmart to clean them out of all their cardboard boxes and packing tape…. We were out of there three days later with a friend offering to drive the moving van if I bought him a plane ticket back home. Sounded great to me.

It was very hard for me to leave the state that God had brought me to. I had many precious, close friends, a wonderful church, and memories of seeing God's hands on my life. It was hard to leave two sweet, precious elderly ladies who were wonderful "moms" to me. I am still in contact with friends from down there. We had become a family. Again, I adjusted to another life style, this time, far busier because my daughter and her children were very close. It was a joy to make supper for them and be an active part of their lives.

But the first thing I needed to do was to find a doctor. I did some research, but nothing "clicked". One day, as we were exploring the new city, I seen a clinic sign and a doctor's name struck me and stuck in my mind. The next day, I called the number and made an appointment with him. And went to it. He and I got along very well. He listened, and did some blood work. When his nurse called me with the lab results, she said, "honey chile, yer a lil bit anemic. I ain't never seen nothin' like it. Have ya'll ever thought about maybe takin' a little bit a iron?" I said, "Ma'am, I have been taking (stated the amount) ever since I was in fourth grade. As is recorded in my medical history… This is the problem, and the reason I came in." "Well, I just don't have any idea what you should be doin'." "Well, then, I am very thankful that you're not the doctor." If you would please transfer me to the appointment desk, we will see what he thinks."

When I met with the doctor, he repeated what the doctors had said before. I told him I was aware that I didn't have much time left. He said now it was closer to six weeks and didn't know how I kept going. (Apparently being a stubborn Swede still helps …) I told him what all the other doctors, clinics, and hospitals had said. He said, "I don't care what anyone says. I've made an appointment for you at the cancer treatment center on Monday. You be there, and I'll make sure your insurance covers it. I'm not going to sit here and watch you die." Thank You Lord for that man!!! For a few months, I went regularly, and my bone marrow began to function properly again, and praises to God, for the first time in my life, I was no longer anemic! And being gluten free had let the bleeding ulcers heal. God knew exactly which doctor to send me to and where he was. He knew the one who had the knowledge and courage to stand up to the world. God used him to save my life. I was beginning to feel alive and more energetic again. God knew I would need energy and strength. He had a couple of wonderful surprises for me.

The day came when I received a call from an out of state number that looked familiar. I answered it, and it was one of the boys who had lived with me, while their cousin had custody quite a few years before. He was going through a rough spot in his life, and asked if he could come "home". "Of course." I said, and a few days later, I picked him up at the bus depot. Sometimes, life is like riding a bucking horse. No matter how hard you try to stay on, sometimes you still get thrown out of the saddle. After he had been there for a few months, his older brother had a similar situation, so he and his two beautiful daughters came to live with us also. I was extremely blessed to get to know my boys again, see the men that they had grown up to be, and to be there for them when they needed me. I was thankful to spend a lot of time with my precious grandchildren. The days flew by, and while I enjoyed my life, I was never comfortable there. I am not a city girl, I get claustrophobic when surrounded by buildings and not enough privacy to even open a window for a bit of fresh air. After two years of this, God started to put a longing for something else in my soul. The boys were settled, and had found good jobs, and one had a new relationship that worked out very well. His girls liked her, and she appreciated them. I was very happy for them. But me - I was getting to the "anywhere but here" moment.

One day my sister called, she was the executor of our parents' estate. Daddy had passed away a few weeks before, and she wanted to know if I was interested in "the forty". I was speechless. When Dad had sold the farm and retired, he had kept the forty and built a small, modest house on it and moved up there. My heart stopped for a minute, and I said, "WHAT???" She said, "You don't have to take it! It was just a thought." "NO!!! I want it! PLEASE don't sell it to someone else!" "OK. When can you move up there and take possession? The renters are moving out soon." I said, "I want it. I'll talk to my Heavenly Father, and my husband. And get back to you."

Every day, I would ask Him, "Today?" "No." "Ok." This went on for quite a while. But I never gave up hope, knowing I was in His hands. Then came the day when I asked Him "Today?", and He said, "YES, NOW." I called my friend, the same realtor we had bought it from, and asked her to list it. It was photographed and contracts signed on Thursday, listed early Friday morning, showed it Saturday and Sunday, multiple times, and an offer was submitted and signed on Monday. If anything is in His will, and in His timing, it always works out perfectly. And everyone was surprised except me. (FYI… if you are selling a house, it never hurts to have a couple of loaves of fresh baked, hot, homemade bread on the kitchen counter, and a fresh pot of coffee. Smells homey and inviting.…)

Again… back to cleaning out local stores supplies of cardboard boxes and packing tape. This time I had family to help. One of my "sons" decided to move up with us and volunteered to drive the moving van. We didn't know why God put this in his heart, but God had a plan… People I hardly knew came to help. It was actually fun this time. While I knew I was going to miss my family, I knew they would be fine. My son and daughter had gone through their storms and came out on the other side, They were in solid relationships with God and each other. My grandchildren were all doing well. God put me there to get medical care, and to help the kids through bumpy stretches in their lives. Now. He was taking me home, and I couldn't hold back my tears of joy.

As we headed out, I thanked God for caring about me, and for His uncountable blessings. It was a wonderfully peaceful drive home. This son had only been in a couple of states before, so he was excited every time we crossed a state line. For me, it was a "check", one down a few more to go… He had no idea why God had sent him with us. But a couple of months later, we discovered that God knew exactly where "his other half was." They were married and have been happy together ever since. Thank You Lord for knowing each of Your children so well. It reminds me of when my daughter told me that life was like sitting under a glass table and watching someone put a puzzle together. She said, "God is putting the puzzle together, and we're underneath watching. We can't see the whole picture, but we can see it coming together."

We arrived in the spring of 2017. As far as I understand, it was "the year of jubilee". Leviticus 25:8-11. "It shall be a jubilee for you; you shall be returned to your family property and to your own clan." God gave me back the earthly haven of my heart. And I was reunited with the son of my heart.

When this amazing, special little boy was born, everyone smiled who seen him. He was the New Year's baby in our small town and was one of those little guys who engaged everyone who seen him. My kids loved playing with him, and he was with my family and cousins a great deal of the time. My mother couldn't see him without smiling. Or picking him up. And neither could I. And yet, he was never "spoiled". Even as a little boy, he enjoyed working hard on the farm. He had grown up as one of our family. He is the one that when I was driving back and forth from the east coast – before GPS, he would write out the trip with specific highway intersections, on and off ramp details and fully expected me to call him from a payphone every time I stopped for gas. Before cell phones, we had payphones and "phone cards". He was just out of high school then. He always kept track of me, and as soon as cell phones came in, he went with me to make sure I got a good one. A few people laughed at his protectiveness of me. They said, "Your 'mother hen' instincts must have rubbed off on him. Praise God that they did, and he has sons who are as amazing as their wonderful Daddy.

When God was moving me south, he had told me that I would be back. And that he would "keep all my stuff" including my winter coat – which he called my "blueberry coat", snowmobile boots, and sewing machine. I said, "Why would I ever come back? God's moving me down there. I won't go against His will." He said, "You'll see, you'll be back…" Ohhh, I should have listened, he was right. Every time there has been a major decision in my life, he has always been right. Everything 'is for a season', and some seasons last longer than others. And there's a reason for every season.

He was on the phone with me at least half of the trip. He called me and warned me to get off at "the next exit you see a motel, because there's a bad snowstorm coming." He was right. Glad I had listened to him. He has taken off work and driven hundreds of miles and many hours to come get me when something dreadful had happened. He recruited two other family members to come with him because he didn't want me to have to drive home alone. He has stayed up until 2:30 in the morning for over a year, talking to me to be sure I was safe, knowing that he had to leave for work in a few short hours. He has always been there for me, and I thank God for him, and pray that God will bless him greatly. He has been a huge blessing except when he picked me up and sat me on top of a nearly 5' barn fan that I couldn't figure out how to get down from. Which was why he put me up there in the first place. He is full of mischief and shenanigans also… When people see us together, they assume he is my son. Recently, I introduced him to some friends of mine as my extra blessing son, purely a gift straight from God. I was asked, "Not biological?" My son answered before I could. "Might as well be." And my friends stared back and forth from him to me. One said, "This is so strange. You look alike, you walk alike, you move alike, you sure do look like mother and son." We both smiled and said, "yes, we do." He said, "The stork must have delivered him to the wrong house."

I was extremely blessed to be able to bring his son to see my mother while she was still able to see him, and I treasure the pictures of them together. There are not enough words in any language to describe her love for him, and her happiness to see "her grandson".

This "son" was and always will be an amazing gift from God. When we arrived, he met me at the hotel where we were going to stay until we got everything unpacked and ready to move in. He had the keys, but before we opened the door and walked into my "new" house, we prayed and dedicated it to our Lord and Savior. What a joyful moment. Kind of funny, both of my boys – the one up here, and the one who drove the truck, have the same name. They worked well together, and the truck was unloaded.

And, with never ending praise, I am home. Truly home. God brought me through all the storms of life, knowing that in His perfect timing, He was going to bring me back to the only place I have ever felt total, perfect peace. Every day I see the beauty and peace of this place, I still cry in thankfulness and joy to my Heavenly Father.

Am I living a boring Christian life? NO! Am I grateful to be alive and in His service? YES! And I am equally certain that the ride isn't over. I have been told that I am 'uber' religious, and I smile. I know His word is true, and I know that I am extremely blessed to be alive. He still has a purpose and a plan for me. My work isn't done. When it is done, I won't be here. I get to go to my forever home. And. It won't involve more cardboard boxes and packing tape! That will be someone else's problem!

Until that moment, I will serve Him and fully live the life He has given me for His glory. I believe that He has always wanted me to know that I was His child - greatly loved and appreciated, open and willing to receive His best. And – to be able to love and serve Him joyfully, knowing that He will never send me down a wrong road. I'm praying hard that the story of my life will bring you closer to the One who loves you more than anyone else ever could, who wants to provide for you, shelter you, and bless you greatly. I can step out in faith knowing that my life is in the hands of the One who 'never slumbers or sleeps'. Thank You Father, Jesus, and Holy Spirit. I am a new creation in Christ. My sins are washed away; because Jesus paid the ultimate price, washed me clean, and redeemed me from a life of sorrow, shame, and regrets. THANK YOU, LORD JESUS, FOR THINKING THAT I WAS WORTH DYING FOR!

www.ingramcontent.com/pod-product-compliance
Lightning Source LLC
LaVergne TN
LVHW011957070526
838202LV00054B/4952